Don't Faint

Don't Faint

Help for Hurting Pastors and Their Families

Rev. Dr. Harry L. Seawright

To order additional copies of this book, contact:
Xlibris Corporation
1-888-795-4274
www.Xlibris.com
Orders@Xlibris.com
104894

CONTENTS

DEDICATION

In loving memory of my parents,

Mary Leatha Seawright
and
Joe Nathan Seawright,

two people who did not faint.

COMMENTS FROM REVIEWERS

"Don't Faint: Help for Hurting Pastors and Their Families, is very moving and offers practical suggestions for persons in ministry. It is clear that certain themes have been woven in Dr. Seawright's life from the beginning. It almost suggests a degree of predestination. This is an excellent book and needs to get in the hand of every Christian."

Rev. Dr. Lee P. Washington, Pastor
Reid Temple AME Church
Glendale, Maryland

"Rev. Harry L. Seawright's book reveals to clergy how to serve God when you are suffering. Rev. Seawright's spiritual life and pastoral experience have been enriched through coping with pain. He shares that faithful friends, colleagues, family and God's love have enabled him to understand the biblical concepts of faith and hope. Rev. Seawright's life and ministry give credibility with pastors who may be paralyzed by pain. This book is a must read, if you feel spiritually and physically exhausted. Remember, " *Don't Faint* "God does heal, but not at our command."

Rev. Kenneth H. Hill, PhD
Presiding Elder
13th Episcopal District
African Methodist Episcopal Church

"You think you know a person – until you read their story. For Harry L. Seawright, God is in the details. *"Don't Faint: Help for Hurting Pastors and their Families"* is memoir, testimony and aspiration. The aim of his writing, he says, is to encourage fellow pastors on their journey; indeed he does. With three and a half decades in ministry and successful pastorates, Dr. Seawright is transparent enough to reveal an authentic real-time witness. With a degree, "magna cum laude" from the proverbial *University of Hard Knocks*, as well as the mind-stretching, opportunity-enhancing, bona fide degrees from the halls of academe, Seawright demonstrates that he is duly qualified to teach others. He speaks with passion from his own life-story to the realities of the human condition: doubt about the calling, lack of sufficient resources, personal trials, and life-threatening health challenges. This is the practical meaning of pathos. With a thankful heart, Dr. Seawright is tactfully self-deprecating but driven, coupled with bold ambition for a phenomenal future. If we are looking for answers in a "how to" book about the pastorate, we just might miss the value of Dr. Seawright's insights. The exhortation here is to encourage and inspire in fellow members of "the cloth" steadfast reliance upon the extraordinary faithfulness of our gracious, loving God. Mission accomplished."

Adam Jefferson Richardson, Jr.
115th Bishop in the African Methodist Episcopal Church

"Perhaps the most amazing aspect of this work is that the author, a pastor, who aspires to become a bishop in his denomination, has the courage to write a religious psycho-social autobiography revealing not only his divine calling but his imperfect humanity. In so doing, however, he demonstrates how pastors can faithfully minster through hurt, pain and suffering by availing themselves of not only the resources of their faith but also by being vulnerable enough to understand that peer groups and counselors are also instruments of God in helping pastors care for themselves, their families and their congregations. The techniques for self care indicated by Dr. Seawright are very insightful in helping pastors maintain health, set boundaries and manage stress. This is a book with which all pastors can identify and by which they can be guided in their pursuit of a faithful and authentic ministry."

Cameron W. Byrd, D.Min,
Recurring Adjunct Professor of Pastoral Care
Howard University School of Divinity

Pastor Harry Seawright has made a great contribution to freeing the pulpit & the pew from the pressure of pretense. All healing begins with truth & is sustained by faith. In that light, the Seawright story is medicine for the soul. Read it, and faint not.

Rev. Dr. Michele Balamani Silvera,
Founder/Director Baraka Counseling Center

Author: Dancing on Our Graves: Healing the Hearts & Souls of Women

FOREWORD

I AM PLEASED that Rev. Dr. Harry Seawright decided to write a book titled, *Don't Faint: Help for Hurting Pastors and Their Families,* that addresses the pain, the hurt, the struggles, the joys and the happiness of being called into the Pastoral Ministry. It is not often that a prominent Pastor, Minister, candidate for Bishop tells his story so vividly to help pastors, ministers and their families, especially those who are on the edge of hopelessness and are giving up because it is too difficult to balance the many roles they have to play daily. The writer shares personal experiences on and how he and his family were able to make it through some of the toughest times of his life. Through these experiences, it is evident that there is a God, a God that is faithful to His children. Wisdom learned from these experiences will make you cry, will make you laugh, but most of all will provide you with a sense of hopefulness and a sense of renewal; it will make you fall in love with Christ all over again.

Dr. Harry Seawright's life is a wonderful example of how one can overcome any obstacle. All you have to do is put all your trust in God. This Pastor, author, entrepreneur was raised in a rural southern town, Swansea, South Carolina. He referred to his early years as, "poverty years of his life". His parents were sharecroppers; and, at an early age, Dr. Seawright lost his father which left his mother to raise seven children. Through the Grace of God he was able to work his way through school and move from poverty to accomplishment. Even through this journey, there were hurt and pain. God placed people and resources in his path that allowed him to graduate from Benedict College, where he received a Business Administration degree, Howard University School of Divinity, where he received a Master in

Divinity and Doctor in Ministry degrees. He was blessed to attend Oxford University in Oxford, England. His first book was published in 1996, *"More than Bricks and Mortar: Building a Church without Losing Your Mind"*.

Dr. Seawright has faced challenges with his family, health, ministry, finances, and had to deal with inner struggles . . . but his faith in God, Jesus Christ and the Holy Spirit helped him through it all. Each step on his journey made him a stronger, faithful, and a humble servant of God. He took on a leadership role at an early age and became a pastor at the age of twenty-one.

He is married to Rev. Sherita Moon Seawright, has two children, Shari and Matthew; and a grandson, Cameron. A Pastor's family not only feels, but experiences the pain and hurt; but it is remarkable how this family was able to stick together, set boundaries, and overcome situations that were placed before them. Today, Dr. Seawright is the Senior Pastor of Union Bethel AME Church in Brandywine, Maryland; Candidate for Bishop, Forty-ninth Session of the General Conference of the AME Church, an Executive Leader in the 2nd District of the Washington Conference, Entrepreneur and founder of HLS Consulting, Inc., We KLEEN, Inc., Prestigious Property Management, Inc. and Bethel House, Inc..

This book demonstrates the life of Dr. Seawright as a beacon of light that will help Pastors see during the dark times in their journey. *Don't Faint: Help for Hurting Pastors and Their Families*, will inspire the reader to continue on the path that God has destined for their lives. The title epitomizes the author's personal struggle and throughout the book, he pours out his heart and becomes transparent. He allows the reader to feel his hurts and pains, yet share his joy as he provides valuable lessons that will encourage you to remain steadfast in this journey that we call Ministry.

I write this Foreword with the prayer that all who read this book will be inspired, motivated, rejuvenated and challenged to fulfill God's will. God has a plan and a purpose for your life. If God has called you to be a Pastor or as Dr. Seawright says, "a person of the Cloth", God will provide you with everything that you need. Not only will he provide, but he will comfort you through your losses, he will heal your pains, he will deliver you from church wounds, and he will strengthen your family. And most of all God will love you and send special people in your life at different times to support you on your journey.

Rev. Valdes Snipes-Bennett, PhD

ACKNOWLEDGEMENTS

I N THE WORDS of the late Dr. Benjamin E. Mays, "Lord, the people have driven me on". In his book of the same title, he looked back over his life and named many of the people who helped him throughout his life. I wish to do the same. I am so grateful for the many persons who have played significant roles in my life. To all the people who prayed for me, and those who continue to pray for me. I am a strong believer in the power of prayer and I thank God for my daily prayer partner, Sherita, my wife, friend and strongest supporter. I am so grateful for the love, trust and bond we have shared over the past thirty-five years. We have been blessed in our fruitfulness with Shari, Matthew and our grandson, Cameron. I am grateful for the support of family and friends, church families with whom I have shared my life and ministry. Other prayer partners who prayed with me without fail on a daily basis: my son, Harry Matthew Seawright, Rev. R. Hamilton Crump, Bro. Kevin Carter, Bro. Micheal Foskey and Bro. E. Cornell Alexander. I am grateful for the International Prayer Line Ministry family who prays with me daily by phone, 6:00 am, Monday thru Saturday, and the Intercessory Prayer Ministry of Union Bethel church who leads several sessions of intercessory prayer during the week between our two locations.

I wish to give special thanks to the African Methodist Episcopal (AME) Church for the opportunities and privileges that allowed me to be an instrument of God throughout the world. I am grateful for the fond memories of friends like the late Dr. Walter L. Hildebrand, Dr. William R. Porter, Rev. Henry Harper, Dr. Joseph C. McKinney, and Dr. Edgar James. I am also grateful for my Bishop and Episcopal Supervisor, the Right Reverend Adam J. and Mrs. Connie S. Richardson, Presiding Elder Goodwin and

Mrs. Cynthia Douglas, Presiding Elder George and Dr. Virginia Manning, and my former Presiding Elders and all Pastors. I would like to acknowledge other Bishops, Presiding Elders, Pastors and Laity of the AME Church who have supported me. I also wish to thank my support group and my confidantes, the Reverends Dessie Carter and Arthur Glover, my god-sister, Mrs. Bettye Sydnor, and my armor bearers. To all of my close Pastoral friends, ministers, Fathers and Mothers in the ministry, lay people, and the many ecumenical friends I have gained outside of the AME Church. I have chosen not to list names to avoid the possibility of leaving someone's name out; but you know who you are. I appreciate all your support throughout the years.

I am grateful to my Union Bethel African Methodist Episcopal Church family, business partners, sons and daughters in Ministry, my past and present administrative staff personnel, ministerial staff members, and the leadership in the form of Stewards, Trustees, Stewardesses, Class Leaders, Missionaries, Commission Chairs, and ministries and organization leaders. I am grateful to the administrative and management personnel, as well as the employees of We Kleen, Inc., Prestigious Property Management, Inc. and HLS Consulting, Inc., Bethel House, Inc., Unity Economic Development Corp., F.O.C.U.S., Inc. (For Our Children's Unity School) and the Committee to Elect Seawright for Bishop. I thank my first editor, Dr. Bettye Bellamy, editorial assistant, Ms. Arlene Duckett, and my present editor, Dr. Valdes Snipes-Bennett. Their invaluable input, suggestions and editing have been superb. Thanks for encouraging me and staying on my case to remain focused and meet deadlines.

To the members of my publishing team from Xlibris Publishing Company, thanks for your patience, guidance and consistent attention to details and deadlines.

I am grateful to God Almighty, Jesus Christ, my friend and Savior, the Holy Spirit my guide and teacher, comforter and healer, for all the love, hope, grace, mercy and power provided throughout my life. Thanks for helping me navigate through all the pathways, roads, bridges, airways, byways, wildernesses, adventures and tests. Words cannot fully express my gratitude for all You have done. Thank you.

INTRODUCTION

PAIN IS REAL. Hurt is devastating, and the effects can linger long after the wounds seem to have healed. In fact, the aftereffects can be seen in a number of ways: decline in health, rebellious children, depression, financial distress, divorce, and prolonged grief after the death of loved ones. God has created each person with the hope of being able to deal with the *real* issues of life. We are faced with issues, such as the physical pain of affliction and the mental agony of betrayal, rejection, embarrassment, depression, sin, and death. I am a pastor with a little over thirty years of experience, nearly thirty-five years as a minister, almost thirty years of marriage, the rearing of two children who are now adults (Glory be to God!), a precocious grandchild who is the joy of my life, and over fifty "sons and daughters" to whom I've served as a mentor in the ministry. Our God is an awesome God, and I have witnessed the power of the ministry in not only my life but also in the lives of others. My friendships and association with a countless number of ministers from *all* walks of life have given me much insight regarding the title of this book. I have interacted with pastors and their families, and because of my firsthand knowledge, I have observed their pain of enduring pastoral appointments and how it weighed on their health, marriages, children, and other relationships that spilled over into their churches. I have been a witness to pastors who wanted to quit and to those who did quit because of the hopelessness and pain they encountered.

I have been exceedingly blessed in my pastoral ministry in that I am still ministering and continuing to get a genuine sense of enjoyment from doing so. However, this Christian journey has not been without its share of ups and downs. The hazards of pastoral ministry should come with a warning label similar to what we find on medical prescriptions. Anyone who is serious about being a pastor needs to know that it does have side effects. How you deal with those side effects will either make you or break you.

After 35 years of ministry and reflecting upon those years, prayerfully, I am asking the question, "What can I do to encourage pastors who are at the edge of hopelessness and are ready to throw in the towel or those dealing with the pain of trying to balance family life and their congregation?" It is out of this concern and love for my sisters and brothers of the cloth and their families that I come to offer words of wisdom that have enabled me to make it thus far.

If one pastor can be rejuvenated as a result of this book or one pastoral family can remain hopeful and continue to believe in the possibilities of God and what He can do through the church, then my work will not be in vain. Writing a book is quite a task. The idea for this book came as an inspiration to me several years ago but was placed on the back burner as new visions and revelations began to manifest in my life and ministry. Of course, I will only share information that will not violate the trust and sanctity of those persons who have shared personal encounters of the pain, the hurt, and the disappointments of ministry.

People who know me know that I am quick to lend a listening ear and offer a prayer for those who need one. Aren't ministers/pastors supposed to do this? I have become prayer partners with many persons as we work to encourage each other in the ministry, whether lay or pastoral. After some recent disappointments, setbacks, and looking back over my life, I decided to dig out my old notes and complete the process of writing this book. I am hopeful that it will serve as a beacon to you and as a reminder that you are neither the first nor the last to encounter the *side effects* of ministry. The ministry, at times, can make one feel so inadequate and limited that one will become consumed with self-doubt and question God's calling on his or her life. Again, my fellow pastors, I want you to know that there are others who are fighting similar battles; dealing with similar struggles of inadequacy; trying hard to keep everything in perspective; seeking God's grace, love, and mercy; praying; fasting; and hoping for a better and brighter tomorrow. Remember this as we press forward: if God brought us to it, He and only He will see us through it.

There are battles to fight, jealousies to deal with, hating and distrust we must stand against. Not only that, there are temptations, hidden fears to overcome, political issues and concerns in the church as well as outside of the church that must be dealt with constantly. In addition to dealing with the negative issues, we have to continue to reach souls that need to be saved, preach sermons that need to be preached, visit the sick and the shut-in, preside at funerals, perform weddings and baptismal ceremonies. You will have meetings and more meetings to attend. Then there is the issue of survival as a pastor: issues of integrity, truth, seeking of wholeness and holiness for self and others. There will be tests and challenges that only you can understand while wishing that others could. You will encounter frowns and smirks on faces that you must ignore or overcome, gestures that only you can see, insults that only you can relate to, and callous remarks that cut to your very core! There are frustrations that no one knows about but you and God. I hope, as you read this book, it will encourage you to keep holding onto God's unchanging hands and remind you that you did not miss your calling.

Whether you have a large church or a small church, whether you have an affluent church or one with modest means, whether you are a member of a denomination or are nondenominational, the pain is usually the same for pastors, ministers, and their families. We all hurt. We all want to be appreciated, we all want to be loved, and we all want to be abundantly blessed by God. We want a nice home for our families. We all want job security.

We want our congregation to love and respect our family. We want people to understand that we have a need for self-care, a need for rest, and a need for help with the many, many demands and tasks of the ministry.

I will attempt to realistically share some of the challenges I have faced as a pastor without embarrassing my family or breaching the confidentiality of those who have confided in me. The intent of this book is to offer encouragement, give hope for those who have reached a level of hopelessness, and provide a sense of renewal for those who feel the battle is too fierce or the odds are stacked too high against them or both. This book is not based on scholarly research, but personal accounts.

Issues and Concerns

What do you do when a spouse informs you that she does not feel appreciated at the church and does not want to go back? What do you do when your children tell you they hate church and the people within it? What do you do when just a few faithful and loyal supporters show up at the pastoral appreciation service? What do you do when your work is always compared to the former pastor and it never seems to measure up? What do you do when membership decreases and your leadership skills are questioned? What do you do when your vision is DOA (dead on arrival) by the naysayers and the mean-spirited? What do you do when someone thinks he or she can do your job better than you can because they have been the "unofficial" pastor down through the years? What do you do when the church becomes divided?

How do you respond when your spouse is appreciated more than you are or you are liked more than your spouse? How do you respond when your children overhear someone talking negatively about you? How do you respond when the congregation wants your children involved with every youth activity sponsored at the church? How do you explain to your children that there will be no Christmas gifts because the church furnace broke and the pastor's salary was used to fix the furnace? How do you respond when the church and you are at an impasse when it comes to your compensation?

What happens when a pastor becomes sick and the major concern of the church leadership is how quickly can they get another pastor? What do you do when your spouse is criticized for being too involved or not involved enough? What happens when pastors suffer physical and verbal abuse from members of the congregation? What happens when allegations of physical, verbal, and sexual abuse are leveled at your own home?

Where do you go for encouragement? Where do you go for renewal? Where do you go when the first family needs privacy? Where does the pastor, spouse, or children go when they are hurting?

Through some personal and trying experiences, I will share how I and many others made it through some extreme and extenuating circumstances as pastors and families. Through it all, there is nothing like being kept by God's grace.

CHAPTER ONE

Fields of Cotton, Corn, and Beans
My Formative Years

"I knew you before I formed you in your mother's womb. Before you were born I set you apart and appointed you as my prophet to the nations." "O Sovereign LORD," I said, "I can't speak for you! I'm too young!" The LORD replied, "Don't say, 'I'm too young,' for you must go wherever I send you and say whatever I tell you. And don't be afraid of the people, for I will be with you and will protect you. I, the LORD, have spoken!" (Jeremiah 1: 4-8)

FROM THE COTTON, corn, and bean fields of rural South Carolina to the academic and scholarly halls of Benedict College in Columbia, South Carolina; Howard University School of Divinity in Washington, DC; University of District of Columbia (Mortuary Science); Oxford University in Oxford, England; Wharton School of Business (Leadership Development Program); University of Pennsylvania; appointed for six years to the Prince George's Community College Board of Trustees of Largo, Maryland; and from the pulpit of Prodigal African Methodist Episcopal Church in Swansea, South Carolina to major pulpits around the world, the Lord has brought me from a mighty long way. In the Bible, there are scriptures that speak of planting seeds. Jesus used several parables about planting seeds to convey valuable life lessons. One that comes to mind is Matthew 13:24.

He said, "The kingdom of heaven is like a good man who sowed good seed in his field" (NIV Bible). Growing up on a farm, I am very familiar with planting seeds. I believe that success begins in the mind as a small seed that needs to be nurtured with love, always encouraged, and given a commitment of prayer by ourselves and from those persons who surround us. This is why it is so important to align ourselves with righteous and godly people. We all need to be around people who will speak power and encouragement into our lives. It was during my early and formative years that I started dreaming of having a better life and becoming a better person. By the time I declared in the fifth grade that I was going to become a mortician, I knew that life offered great possibilities. While laboring in the fields and working other menial jobs, even as a young child, I knew those jobs were just stepping-stones to a better and more promising life. They became the foundational means to assist me with developing the character and the intestinal fortitude needed to make it in today's society. These jobs helped me develop strong work ethics, an understanding of the value of money, and the ability to persevere in the toughest of times. I am truly grateful that I learned valuable survival skills through the discipline of hard work. Those skills have helped me to endure many difficult challenges in my later life. I am even more grateful that I had a mother who believed in the ethic of work and would not take no for an answer when it came to working and making a living for her family. Widowed at the age of forty-one when my father, Joe Nathan Seawright, passed away at the young age of forty-five due to complications of heart disease and stroke, my mother, Mary Leatha Seawright, continued as a single parent to provide for and instill a positive sense of direction for her seven children. A domestic worker with only a ninth grade education, my mother continued to push her children to excel. One sibling at the time, Dorothy (deceased), was married with two children, and another sibling, Louise, who had just graduated from high school, was

REV. DR. HARRY L. SEAWRIGHT

working in New York on a sleep-in job. She was employed by a family as a domestic worker, and part of her pay was that they provided her with room and board. During this difficult time, my mom had five children (Emma Ruth, who is now deceased; Joseph Daniel; Ernest Frank; Eugene; and me) between the ages of five and seventeen at home who needed her assistance. As sharecroppers, the outlook was pretty bleak. My father, who had a third grade education and worked as a sharecropper all his life, did not have any savings when he died. That was typical of black families in the South. Mom had no funds, and social security paid only $17 per child to the youngest three children. At such a young and tender age, I, along with my siblings, had to find jobs and contribute to the financial well-being of the family. Therefore, we started to work in the fields, picking cotton, beans, gathering corn and other vegetables.

During those "poverty years of my life" as I refer to them today, I knew life had more to offer than cotton, corn, and bean fields. As a sharecropper, my mother was forced off the property since my father was no longer alive to farm the land. My parents had lived in the same house for almost twenty years. Even though it was nothing more than a three-room shotgun shack, it was devastating having to leave the only home I had ever known. My mother with five children was forced to move from house to house over the next several years. I remember that in a span of eight years, we moved to five different houses in which none of them had indoor bathrooms or running water. They were dilapidated buildings that had holes in the walls, broken windows, and leaky roofs. We, as a family, were so proud when my mother was able to save enough money to purchase an acre of land and borrow enough to build a two-bedroom house. It too had no indoor plumbing or running water. It did not matter; it was ours. I vividly remember this milestone in my life and the sense of pride I felt when we moved into our own place. No more moving, plus my three brothers and I had a bedroom we shared. My mother had her bedroom, and my sister slept in the living room. God is good!

This spirit of ownership was seared in my brain, and I vowed that one day I would buy me a house. Moving into this house brought back some stability to our family. Once again, we finally had some place we could call home. Growing up, I had the usual "normal" life of a poor black child growing up in a racist society. I was quite spoiled by my mother and had a lot of cousins who spent summers at our house. I had many friends, playmates, a whole lot of nieces and nephews who were a little younger than me. There were no traumatic, earthshaking happenings that caused unusual pain in my life. Being the youngest child, I was afforded several opportunities that my older siblings were not given. During the summer, I would go to West Columbia, South Carolina, and spend the summer with my sister Louise and her husband, David, and their three children. I became their babysitter. From this experience, I was able to see firsthand a *nuclear family*. My brother-in-law was a good strong husband and father who cherished his family. My sister was hardworking and smart and, like our mother, wanted only the best for her family. They modeled, for many, what a real family looked and felt like. I picked up many family values from staying with them during the summers throughout my early years. Because of this, I was determined to emulate what I observed in their family structure when blessed with a family of my own.

My mother, with some reluctance, allowed me to elevate my age on job applications. I sought employment beyond the fields and entered into the workforce, landing my first summer job at age fourteen at the South Carolina State Mental Hospital—a facility for the mentally insane. I worked as a nurse's aide. Following that experience, my next job was on the army base at Fort Jackson, South Carolina. My duties there were to separate soiled linen for the hospital. This job ended after I was threatened, bullied, and intimidated by a guy much larger and a little older. With the help of my oldest brother-in-law, John Lee (Dorothy's husband), I then got a job as a truck loader. Not only did John Lee help me get this job, he was a stable force in my life and taught me many things about manhood and, like David (also known as Junior), taught me how to take care of a family. I will never forget that John Lee taught me how to tie a necktie. I worked at this job as a truck loader for six years, after school and during the summers, even while I was in college. When times were slow at the trucking company, I worked as a short-order cook, dishwasher, french fry cutter, cleaning technician, a mail handler with the US Postal Service, and while I was still in high school, I drove a school bus.

It was my sister Louise who once told me that when you work and make your own money, you can buy what you want. Those words left an indelible impression with me. I worked and saved my money to buy what I wanted. At the age of sixteen, I purchased my first car; and by the age of eighteen, I purchased my third car—a brand-new 1974 Chevrolet Nova. As I was preparing to graduate from high school, I knew I wanted to go to a trade school to become a plumber. College, for me, was out of the question. Also, I did not have any money to go to college. I don't recall anyone from my family or high school encouraging me to go to college. My grades were average, and I did not do well on the SAT. I was more focused on working and paying my way than anything else. I wanted to have my own money and help my mother as much as possible. However, I had a yearning to do something to improve myself. I had scored high on an electronics inventory test and was strongly pursued by Bell and Howell Electronics School in Atlanta, Georgia. It was at that time my desire to be a plumber surpassed the desire to deal with electronics. One of my classmates, Diana Ginyard (today an anointed, powerful sister in Christ), suggested that I check out Benedict College where she was planning to attend and told me about the financial aid that was being offered to black students through the state and federal government.

Being a person of prayer and faith, I decided to give it a try, and to my surprise, I was accepted and received enough assistance to cover tuition and the Basic Educational Opportunity Grant (BEOG) covered my room and board. I was totally shocked and elated. I had friends who had participated in the Upward Bound program (a federally funded program that allowed high school students an opportunity to prepare for the rigors of college). I had several older cousins attend and graduate from college. However, no one in my immediate family had done so. Members of my immediate family and some friends laughed at me and reminded me of others who had attempted and failed. I was made fun of by friends and told that Benedict College graduates were not able to find jobs. My mother, sister, and a few people from my church encouraged me to go to college.

With unshakable faith in God and a determination to be and do better, I entered college. It was nothing like I expected. I was away from home for the first time in my life, and though only twenty-one miles away, I had never experienced this type of independence. No one really cared if you went to class. No one was there to tell you to get up, go to class, and do your work. The freedom was more than I was used to. My class schedule consisted of having classes on Monday, Wednesday, and Friday for two hours per day, and all the other time was free. I took a leave of absence from my truck-loading job to get adjusted to college. Did I get adjusted? I learned how to play bid whist, specialized in knowing the time for meals in the cafeteria, and partied with my friends from high school that were also students at Benedict College. At the end of my first semester, to my surprise and by God's grace, I passed two of my three courses and got an incomplete for the third course. I was given the opportunity the next semester to make up the incomplete.

After getting through my first semester of college without getting thrown out, I started consistently praying to God to help me be successful in college. My mother was a member of an organization named *Life Study Fellowship Inc.*, an organization that offered special written prayers for certain situations. Well, I requested a prayer to help me be successful in school. I started praying this prayer my second semester in college and continued to pray it until I graduated. In the second semester, I passed all my courses and even made a B in one class. Once again, God is good. I declared business administration as a major because I remembered looking through a college yearbook and seeing a young man from my high school that had majored in this area. However, the dream of being a mortician continued to lurk in the back of my mind. I also knew a man in Columbia who had a very successful real estate business, and I thought this was really wonderful, but I found out there was no major in college for real estate. I had no desire to teach school, and I had not heard the voice of God calling me to the ministry yet. I liked church and religion but knew I needed a call from God in order to pursue the ministry. I thought majoring in business administration would be the avenue to owning my own business one day. During my second year in college, I had the grade point average to pledge a fraternity. I pledged Alpha Phi Omega National Service Fraternity Inc. Pledging gave me a greater sense of discipline. Earlier I had joined the Gordon-Jenkins Pre-Theological Association, which was a Christian-centered student organization on campus. I also became a member of the campus newspaper staff. My third year of college, I decided to specialize in the area of accounting. As I look back and think about the undisciplined, partying student of my freshman year to the more disciplined and focused student serving God my junior year, my soul looks back in wonder. My God got me over.

College gave me a new sense of purpose. I felt that my life was beginning to take shape. For the first time in my life, I started feeling that I belonged and that God had good things in store for me. I soon learned that I had a speech impediment. My pronunciation and enunciation were not up to standards, and I started working on ways to improve this area in my life. It was not until my first year at Howard University School of Religion that I sought out the assistance of a speech therapist.

During my junior year of college, I heard the voice of God and accepted His call to the ministry. Everyone who knew me greatly encouraged me. When I accepted God's call, the only thing I could think about was a vivid memory of me at the age of four years old while playing on the church grounds of Prodigal AME Church. My great uncle, Abraham Seawright Sr., was saying to me, "Lil boy, you gonna be a preacher one day." On January 23, 1977, at Prodigal AME Church in Swansea, South Carolina, before a packed congregation of family and friends, I preached my initial sermon. This was a major undertaking and started me on a journey that I value more than life itself. The honor of being called and chosen by God has overwhelmed my total existence. I owe it all to God, and to Him I give the glory.

By the time I reached my senior year at Benedict College, not only had I accepted my call to ministry, I was exercising and developing my leadership skills. I was elected president of both the Gordon-Jenkins Pre-Theological Association and Alpha Phi Omega Fraternity. A year and six months after my initial sermon, I was assigned interim pastor of St. Stephens AME Church in St. Matthews, South Carolina. The church was located in the same town as my former high school. One of my fraternity brothers, Rev. Jerry Sanders and Dr. Latta Thomas, a minister and college professor at Benedict College, began to advise and encourage me to start pursuing seminary training.

There was so much going on in my life at the age of twenty that I could hardly comprehend it all. I had just met Ms. Sherita Moon, who would later become my wife. The night before my initial sermon, Sherita and I went on our first date. Meeting

Sherita was an answer to my prayer. I had been praying to God that He would send me a girlfriend who would become my wife. The night of our first date, when I returned to the dormitory, I told my roommate, Jerry Sanders, that I had met the "future Mrs. Harry L. Seawright." Falling in love with Sherita was ordained by God. She had such an encouraging spirit. She was smart, straight A student and very disciplined. She was the second oldest of her three siblings and second to her brother and the oldest of her two sisters. She came from a family of modest means; her father a preacher/pastor and her mother a school teacher and graduate of Benedict College. She accepted me for who I was, and she has never placed herself above me. As I pursued the ministry and continued to fulfill the requirements for my business administration degree in accounting, I began to question getting a degree in business administration. I could not see the connection between business and the ministry. My desire to operate my own business was a dream I did not want to abandon completely, but my call from God to be a minister was stronger. I completed my degree in accounting and graduated from Benedict College in May 1978.

After graduation, I applied to the Interdenominational Theological Center in Atlanta, Georgia, and the Howard University School of Religion in Washington, DC. I continued as the interim pastor at St. Stephens while waiting to hear whether I had been accepted at either school. My college professor and minister, Dr. Thomas, urged me to pursue Howard University. The School of Religion had gotten a new dean, Dr. Lawrence N. Jones. According to Dr. Thomas, "Exciting things were happening there." Wherever I ended up going, it would be difficult leaving St. Stephens AME Church. I was truly enjoying being the interim pastor. I received acceptance letters and scholarships from Howard University and the Interdenominational Theological Center. Howard University's School of Religion offered me a full scholarship whereas the Interdenominational Theological

Center only provided me with a partial scholarship. After much prayer, I informed my mother, family, my friends, Sherita, Bishop Frank M. Reid II, Rev. John L. Davis, my pastor, and the congregation of St. Stephens AME Church that I was going to Howard University School of Religion. There I was, on my way to Washington, DC, where I only knew one person, Sherita's aunt, whom I had only met once. My landlord, Mrs. Hattie Kenly of Columbia, South Carolina, asked me to look up her relatives once I got to Washington, DC. What a blessing that was for me. Her relatives became very good friends and a pillar of support upon my arrival.

A Prayer

August 19, 1978 (Day of Arrival in Washington, DC)

Dear God, You know the way I shall go. You know the plans you have for me, plans to do me good and not harm. I really do need Your help and guidance. I need Your protection, provisions and power as I go forth. Please make my crooked roads straight and my rough places smooth. I am weak, but You are strong. Get the glory out of my life and please help me to be successful. Love, Harry.

CHAPTER TWO

Nothing Beats a Failure, but a Try

I Am on the Battlefield for My Lord

"I left my friends and kindred, Bound for the Promised Land, The Grace of God upon me, The Bible in my hand. In distant lands I trod, Crying sinner come to God; I'm on the battlefield for my Lord." (Written by Thomas A. Dorsey, 1899)

WHEN THE TIME came for me to leave for Washington, DC, it seemed that things began to fall apart! The funds I needed to travel to DC were not available, and everyone that I reached out to—had nothing to loan me. Here I was, ready to go, and there was no money whatsoever. As God would have it, two days before my scheduled departure for Washington, DC, my mother received her first disability income check with back pay from the time she had applied to the present month. The night before this blessing, she and I spent time talking and praying. She prayed and I prayed. Lord, didn't we pray for a miracle? When the check came, we called the check a mighty miracle from God. Because of my mother's great sacrifice, I was able to leave South Carolina and start the next chapter of my life as a student in divinity school in the nation's capital. I was twenty-two years old when I arrived in a city where I knew only one person, with very limited funds, and most of the promises made by Howard University's School of Religion had not materialized. I did receive tuition but no room and board. I ended up renting a room in a boarding house that had rats the size of some cats I had seen in South Carolina. I began to question whether I had made the right decision. With no job in a strange city, once again, I turned to God for mercy.

I wanted to return to South Carolina, but I had quit my job with the trucking company, resigned as interim pastor of St. Stephens AME Church, and here I am with one suitcase, two suits, a car note and, now, monthly rent. At the invitation of one of my divinity school classmates, I immediately joined Reid Temple AME Church. Sister Geneva Watson (she is now deceased) introduced me to her husband, Rev. Kearny Watson—the pastor of Reid Temple AME Church. As a member of Reid Temple, I was surrounded by a caring and loving congregation of people that embraced me. I became good friends with quite a few people there, and those friendships have lasted through the years. Soon after joining the church, my financial situation worsened, and I was down to fifty cents a day for dinner. Thank God for McDonald's that offered fifty-cent hamburgers and a free cup of water. My car was on the verge of being repossessed, and as the rats grew bolder at the boarding house, I desperately needed help.

One Sunday, I went to the altar; so overwhelmed that I yelled out to the Lord, pleading for help. As a result of that outburst, several members of Reid Temple formed a committee chaired by Dr. Avis Pointer to give me ten dollars each, every month, to help me out. This kind gesture provided some financial security and enabled me to buy food, pay my car note, and gave me gas money to look for a job. Fortunately, a room became available in the School of Religion's dormitory, and I was able to leave the rat-infested dwelling that had been home for me. My situation began to improve even more when Sherita's aunt, Mrs. Josephine Oliver, who lived in Washington, DC, spoke to her friend, Mr. Thomas Carter, about my predicament. They were both graduates of Benedict College. Mr. Carter was a neighbor of the treasurer of the African Methodist Episcopal Church, Dr. Joseph C. McKinney. I met with Dr. McKinney, and he informed me that he would employ me for at least two weeks. He needed someone to work on some equipment that he had just received from Kittrell College in North Carolina that had recently closed. After the two weeks, he found more work for me to do. There were times when I emptied the trash, swept the driveway, and did other menial chores. My faith began to wane. Here I was with a college degree, and I was pushing a broom and a mop to support myself. I had to keep telling myself that God was paving the way. Several months later, Dr. McKinney approached me and asked me to work with Allen Travel, a newly formed travel agency through the AME Church. He felt that with my business degree and accounting skills, I would do well. I started keeping the books for the travel agency, and pretty soon, I was asked to assist the bookkeeping department for the AME Church. Remember, just a year or so earlier, I could not see the connection between a degree in business and religion. God was my eyes when I could not see. Some years later, I was promoted to chief accountant, and that appointment turned into twelve years of employment. By working in the finance department, I learned the inner workings of the AME Church. It was during this time that I realized that God will use your most difficult moments to teach you your greatest lessons.

Dr. McKinney became my mentor and a strong supporter as I continued my work toward a degree and my quest in ministry. As the accountant with the church's Finance Department, I was able to attend all the general board meetings and general conferences and had the opportunity to meet bishops and pastors from various churches around the world affiliated with the AME Church. Also, I took on the task of running errands for and transporting the bishops, their wives, the general officers, and other officials of the church from and to the airport, train stations, and hotels during meetings and conferences in the DC area. Through these encounters, I grew to have great respect and admiration for the bishops, general officers, and other dignitaries, especially the ones I had an opportunity to work alongside.

To this day, I hold in the highest esteem the following bishops and their wives whom I have had the privilege and pleasure of serving under: the late Bishop Frank Madison Jr. and Mrs. Irene Reid, the late Bishop Henry Wendell Murph and Mrs. Geraldine Murph, Bishop John Hurst and Dr. Dolly Desselle Adams, Bishop and Mrs. H. Hammel Brookins, Bishop Frederick C. and Dr. Theressa James, Bishop Vinton R. and Mrs. Vivienne Anderson, and Bishop Adam J. and Mrs. Connie S. Richardson. I give a special shout out to the Bishops, general officers and outstanding lay leaders of the AME Church, who inspired and blessed me over the years. During these times, I could not see that God was ordering my every step.

"Nothing beats a failure, but a try." I often heard those words spoken by my mother during my childhood and upbringing. In my frequent phone calls to my mother, she constantly reminded me of how much she was praying for me. I was strengthened and encouraged by her faith. I soon realized that many, many people were praying for me. Reid Temple AME continued to be a springboard for my life. I was surrounded by strong and faith-filled people whom I honor today for their love and support. Because of the prayers and outpouring of support from people I did not know and my mother's words ringing in my ears, I could not give up. *I had to keep trying.* I soon came to love the scripture found in Galatians 6:9-"And let us not become weary in well doing: for in due season we shall reap, if we faint not."

You know God is truly, truly awesome. Just a year later after living in a rat-infested boarding house and with only fifty cents for dinner, I was offered an assistant pastor's position at Pilgrim AME Church in Washington, DC. I was welcomed with open arms by the pastor, Rev. James H. Robinson, and his wonderful wife, Sis. Linda Robinson. The Pilgrim AME Church family was very supportive, encouraging, and nurturing. As an assistant pastor there, I worked along with the church administrator, Bro. Richard Watkins, in the church office, overseeing the financial operations of the church and accompanying the pastor with visiting the sick and the shut-ins and other duties as assigned. When Reverend Robinson was transferred to Ward Memorial AME—the home church of my mentor, Dr. McKinney—I continued to serve as the assistant pastor to Rev. Dr. Gregory Edmond who replaced Reverend Robinson at Pilgrim AME. His family immediately became my family away from home. He and Mrs. Mary Edmond were extremely kind to me. Their sons, Andre and Patrick, became my little brothers. When my funds ran out and I could not pay tuition, room, and board for my last semester at Howard University School of Religion, they opened up their home to me, and I moved in with them until I finished Howard. During these lean financial times, Dr. McKinney gave me the hope and assistance I needed to complete my last semester of seminary training. My faith was further strengthened in the fact that if God be for us, who can be against us?

Today, I praise God for the people who saw something in me when I could not see anything in myself. I am indeed grateful for the friends I met in seminary and the different churches I was fortunate enough to be a member of and, in many instances, where I was able to preach. Several pastors invited me to preach and provided love offerings that were of great assistance in providing needed funds for survival. The late Reverend William R. Porter of Hemingway Memorial AME Church, then in Chapel Oaks, Maryland and the Reverend Dessie Carter of Embry AME Church, College Park, Maryland invited me on a regular basis. Even today some of those churches and parishioners continue to consistently contact me to preach at their churches. I have been blessed. God knows I have been blessed.

I say to any person who is wondering about the possibilities of life, please remember that God has a purpose and plan for everybody's life. That purpose of mind is expanded by the number of steps we are willing to take. I echo the words of Iyanla Vanzant in her book, *Value In the Valley*: "When we step out, the universe will start to participate on our behalf." Difficulties and circumstances will arise; that's life, but keep remembering this fact: "You, dear children, are from God and have overcome them, because the one who is in you is greater than the one in the world" (1 John 4:4, NIV Bible). You will never ever know what you can accomplish until you try. Reverend Lee Cousin a retired Colonel (deceased), who served on my ministerial staff at one of my churches, would say, "Go ahead and jump off the cliff. You just might fly." If I may add, if God is telling you to do so, "jump." He will give you wings. "Nothing beats a failure, but a try."

A Prayer

November 23, 1979

Dear God, I honor You for your great love, direction, hope, and help. I value You and the relationship You have given me. Thanks for answered prayers. Thanks for loving care, grace and mercy. Thank you for using me and preparing my heart, mind and soul to be your instrument. I am so weak at times. I get so frustrated with the cares and worries of life, but I am so glad you are more faithful to me than I am to myself. I pray that You will never give up on me, and please keep bringing me out. Love, Harry.

REV. DR. HARRY L. SEAWRIGHT

CHAPTER THREE

If You Have the Power to Only Believe

"Now faith is the substance of things hoped for, the evidence of things not seen." (Hebrew 11:1)

FAITH TO BELIEVE in God and all His possibilities, faith of a praying mother and faith in one's self are powerful tools. The unshakeable love of family, friends, a devoted wife, children, and a grandchild keeps me going. "To dream the impossible dream, to fight the unbeatable foe, to bear with unbearable sorrow and run where the brave dare not go, . . . and to right the unrightable wrong . . . to reach the unreachable star, this is my quest to follow that star no matter how hopeless, no matter how far." That song, written by Joe Darion, has been one of my favorites ever since I heard it sang at an event over thirty-seven years ago at my high school. Having unshakeable faith was a survival skill, especially if you were black. Growing up in a small rural town in South Carolina, racism was very real, and you encountered it on a daily basis. Blacks were able to survive as long as we stayed in our place. Those who decided to test their fate were dealt with accordingly. As a youngster and as a young man, I heard the horror stories about blacks who didn't know their place. There were stories of blacks being lynched, the homes of blacks being burned to the ground, and blacks fleeing to the North to keep from being killed.

Because of the prevalence of racism, the black church became a focal point in the black community to combat this plague in society. The church was not only the place where we went to worship on Sundays and Wednesday night Bible study and prayer meetings; it was a place where the civil rights movement took hold. It became the gathering place when blacks needed to organize "for the cause." As I reflect on this era of my life, I am also reminded that during this time, I don't remember anyone in my hometown not belonging to the church. There were a few members who did not attend as regularly as others. I also remember someone from the church coming to our house monthly to collect church dues. Paying your church dues consistently assured you of a burial space in the church's cemetery upon your death.

My hometown church, Prodigal AME, was a pivotal force in my life that laid a Christian doctrine in which I continue to espouse to even today. Through all my travels over the years, I have not come across another church named Prodigal. It was and still is today a family church. Prodigal consists of families in the surrounding communities. Everyone was caring, and at times, some members were overly aggressive and competitive, especially when it came to choosing leaders in the church. These types of "church fights" were not often, but they would annoy me beyond belief. However, my church helped mold and shape me into the person I am today. Young people always had a role in the church. We were encouraged to participate in the choir and Sunday school. For every religious holiday, we had to learn and say a speech or participate in the church play. As I left to go to college, they showed how proud they were of me by giving me the money to purchase my books. I was the first person in over two decades to enter the ministry there.

I was saved at the mourner's bench on the second Wednesday in August of 1969 at the age of thirteen. Bishop Nehemiah Rhinehart and his wife, Mother Wilhemina Rhinehart of the Solid Rock Full Gospel Ministries of Washington, DC, returned to their native hometown of Swansea, South Carolina, as the guest pastor for our annual revival. On that hot summer night, I made a commitment to Christ and have been on the battlefield fighting for Him ever since.

My love for the church kept me in the church. I was greatly encouraged to participate in church activities by the Sunday school superintendent and by one of my first Sunday school teachers, the late Julia B. Geiger, who taught me and others the value of serving and doing God's work and placing our lives in His hands. A cousin who was also a Sunday school teacher, the late Marguerite Seawright, took me and other young people of the church to Sunday school conventions, exposing us to other churches and opening doors for other possibilities. My love for church was matched by my love of gospel music. As a young man, when I had money, I would order gospel records through the mail. I grew up listening to gospel quartets: the spirit-filled voices of Edna Gallmon Cooke, Mahalia Jackson, Rev. James Cleveland, and one of my all-time favorite songbirds, Evangelist Shirley Caesar, just to name a few. Gospel music spoke to my spirit and gave me the extra boost I needed to keep pressing on. To me, it spoke to my pain and disappointments, helped me cope with the things I could not change, and gave me strength to believe in the possibilities of God. It was my soul's food and the fuel I needed to get to the next level of godliness.

Growing up fatherless and poor, I tried to live a saved life, and that was a major struggle for me. At the age of eighteen, I became a trustee at my church and president of the Lay Organization at the same time. I remember older members of the congregation telling me that I could do it. Even back then, in the back of my mind, I believed that God was preparing me for the ministry. At that time, I never had the courage or the encouragement to honestly think about it. Prior to getting accepted to college, I had resigned myself to being a good church member and becoming a plumber.

Growing up and going through puberty, dating, trying to understand the importance of life, overcoming fears faced during adolescence, fighting with my brothers and peers, and just maintaining my sanity, I owe my survival to a wonderful God. I remember praying that God would bring me through these years marred in confusion. During these "wonder years," I developed a thirst to learn about the African American race. I started going to my high school library, and I began to check out books on great black leaders and writers covering the black experience. I read about Booker T. Washington, George Washington Carver, Thurgood Marshall, Mary McLeod Bethune, and many, many others. I soon began to learn about historically black colleges and universities. I will never forget the day I picked up a college manual and became fascinated by the history of Howard University. I could hardly believe that there was a black university in the United States with a law school, a school of Religion, and a medical school offering opportunities for black students. I believe a seed was sown that day, and I am forever grateful that an internal flame was ignited. As I was reading about Howard University, I had no idea that one day I would earn two degrees from that wonderful institution. When God's hands are on your life, there is no secret what He can and will do. It was also during my adolescent years that I read the entire New Testament of the Holy Bible. My love for books took me to unknown worlds but, at the same time, caused me to become withdrawn from family and friends. I found myself marching to a different drumbeat. I would rather stay home and read a book than go to a party, movie with friends, or a family outing. I slept with a map of the world on the wall next to my bunk bed. Between the ages of sixteen and eighteen, I would look at that map and dream of places where I wanted to go. As of this writing, I have been to the "Mother Land"—South Africa, West Africa and East Africa on six different occasions. I have traveled to Europe, Canada, Mexico, South America, the

Caribbean islands, and almost all states in the United States. What a mighty God we serve.

I was considered by many to be a model student during high school and received the *Student Citizenship Award* at my high school's graduation in 1974. I was told it was the highest nonacademic award that a student could receive. I felt honored and continue to cherish that recognition today.

A Prayer

May 8, 1980

Dear God, sometimes I wonder what the future holds for me. I wonder sometimes about my weaknesses, limitations, inability to say words I want to say and do things like I want to do. I feel so inadequate at times. But I thank you for Your love, grace, and faithfulness to me. Help me to improve in the areas I can. Help me to stop comparing myself to others and believe in the abilities you gave me. Help me to be faithful to my calling and committed to Your will. Love, Harry

CHAPTER FOUR

Turning Lemons Into Lemonade

A Prayer
August 4, 1998

Dear God, I was reading some of the prayers I wrote earlier and to see what You have done and how You have answered my prayers is mind-boggling. I am so grateful that you have brought me through by grace, mercy, love, assurance and understanding. I still need You like never before. Holy Spirit, I will always be grateful for your love. Bills are being paid; every need is being met. God is Good. Jesus is still sovereign; God is still in control, and I am grateful. Love, Harry

SETBACKS, SETUPS, COMEBACKS, disappointments, heart disease, major lifesaving surgeries—the struggles with different names continued, but the will to overcome the challenges was far greater than anything I have ever encountered.

I was one determined individual who really believed that God had called me to make a difference in this world. As my life continued to evolve, I found myself being extremely busy and very much committed to the ministry. I graduated from Howard University School of Religion in May 1981 and received the distinguished student award, *The Student Most Likely to Excel in the Pastoral Ministry.* My faith continued to be strong and was reinforced by my pastoral appointment to my first church, Payne

Memorial AME in Jessup, Maryland. When Bishop John H. Adams ordained and appointed me to this church in May 1981, my heart was filled with irrepressible joy, and I immediately went to work with a determination that I was going to give God my best. After nine months of serving as the pastor of Payne Memorial AME, Sherita and I were married on February 27, 1982. A year and a half into my two-year appointment at this church, God blessed the congregation with the installation of indoor plumbing. The church had been without such facilities throughout its eighty-seven-year history. These people were beautiful, cooperative and caring; they definitely had a mind to work.

Shortly after getting married, my wife and I expected our first child. Unfortunately, Sherita suffered a miscarriage. As traumatic as this was, we were not defeated, and a few months later, Sherita was pregnant again. As we once again prepared for parenthood, I was assigned to my second church. In May of 1983, I became the pastor of Hemingway Temple AME Church of Washington, DC. The church, located in the inner city, had a notable outreach ministry supporting the needy. There was a soup kitchen already in place, instituted by the previous pastor, the Rev. Ulysees Brooks, and the soup kitchen committee, chaired by Bro. John Cox Sr. Upon my arrival, we began dispensing personal hygiene bags to the homeless, provided free income tax preparation during tax season, paid down the debt of the church, and worked to increase membership through door-to-door evangelism. My wife and I were surrounded by a host of wonderful and gracious members. They are a divine church family who genuinely care about the well-being of people. Once again, I was determined to give God nothing less than my best. I worked along with the church to install air-conditioning and new carpet. Also, we continued to work relentlessly to increase membership. To my disappointment, the membership did not grow as rapidly as we had anticipated. Many of us believed this was a result of where the church was located. After two years, we ventured to move the church to the suburbs of Maryland with the hope of expansion. Unfortunately, due to a lack of funds and overall support, this plan failed. I was disappointed.

This became, to me, my first major setback in my ministry. Up until this time, all that I had envisioned doing as a pastor had been fulfilled. I believed I had the *Midas touch*—everything I touched turned to gold. However, it was with this defeat that I started to question my capabilities as a pastor. I was committed to trying to increase the congregation, but it was not happening. I took it personally. My faith began to diminish, and self-doubt set in. Disillusioned, I enrolled at the University of the District of Columbia (UDC) to pursue a degree in mortuary science. I figured that I needed something else to fill the void I thought was missing from my life as a minister. I thought this would fulfill my long-delayed dream of becoming a mortician. This seemed to be a viable solution to my feelings of inadequacy. Today, it is difficult for me to believe that there was a time in my life when I seriously contemplated walking away from the ministry.

While studying at UDC, Sherita and I purchased our second home in the suburbs of Maryland. We had a beautiful daughter, Shari Nicole, and were awaiting the birth of our son, Harry Matthew. Sherita had a great job with the federal government, and life for us was pretty content as I continued to work toward getting a degree in mortuary science. After three semesters at UDC, in June of 1986, Bishop John Adams issued me my third pastoral assignment to Union Bethel AME Church in Brandywine, Maryland. I had visited Union Bethel, but had very limited knowledge of the church. However, I found myself excited about going there, especially when I realized the church was ripe and ready for growth. Sherita and I were pleasantly surprised to find that the church was just a twelve-minute drive from our newly purchased home. Once again, we were welcomed by an exuberant congregation who was excited about having a young family as the first family of the church. Sherita gave birth to Harry Matthew six months after my appointment. My faith was renewed, and I knew God was orchestrating His plan for my life and ordering my steps.

Almost immediately after arriving at Union Bethel AME, my presiding elder, Dr. Walter L. Hildebrand and the members informed me that they wanted to build a new church. We all understood what a mighty task this would be and the significant challenges we would face, yet we went full steam ahead. Planning committees, building committees, and fund-raising committees were established. We hired an architect, engineers, contractors, consultants, and in the midst of it all, engaged volunteers. Through God's grace, the church membership began to expand, and pretty soon, we had quite a few new members who also embraced the vision of building a new church. For me, I continued to preach, visit the sick, and work to perform all the usual pastoral responsibilities as needed. After five years, the wondrous sanctuary was complete, and to God we give the honor and the glory.

The building of a new Union Bethel AME Church was not without pain, some tears, sacrifices, illnesses, deaths, disappointments, and setbacks along the way. Two months before construction commenced on the new edifice, I was hospitalized and underwent surgery to have my gallbladder removed. It was during this time that I resigned from the AME Church Financial Department to dedicate myself totally to Union Bethel. After six weeks of recuperation, I was back at work with the church and leading the way for the new facility. Life's challenges continued to wear at my soul. During the building of the church in March of 1991, Sherita's mom, Mrs. Aurelia Dillard Moon passed away after being ill. My mother-in-law was a strong, faithful woman who was always encouraging Sherita and me. Her death had a major impact upon our lives. Even though Shari and Matthew were young children at the time of her passing, they did have an opportunity to know their grandmother and were able to reap the benefits of her profound wisdom. Before she passed away, Sherita was often in South Carolina by her bedside.

On one of those occasions, as I recall, construction had stopped on the church! The contractor had walked off the site and was demanding more money, which we did not have, and the bank was refusing to give us another loan. Not only that, with Sherita out of town, I was taking care of the children, and it was not going well. Matthew got up one morning, and as I was assisting him in getting dressed for school, I realized he didn't have any clean underwear. Feeling overwhelmed, I literally began to cry and was ready to throw in the towel. My saving grace was that later that day I had a meeting with Rev. Dr. C. Anthony Muse, and after the meeting, I confided in him and told him of my predicament. He told me to get in his car, and he drove me to the church's construction site. Standing in the middle of the site, in mud and water he prayed with me. Never will I forget a line from that prayer: "God is able to complete that which He has started." My faith was renewed, and my situation began to turn around once again. The following Sunday, the congregation was asked to dig deep and donate $11,000, the amount we needed to complete what God had started. To my pleasant surprise, many members made financial sacrifices, and those that were not prepared to donate during the service ended up bringing checks by my house later that evening. By Monday morning, I had collected a little over $12,000. Construction resumed, and four months later, we were in the building, celebrating the dedication. However, we did not reach that milestone without more struggles and challenges along the way. A week before the dedication of the new sanctuary, the contractors said there was no way that the dedication would occur on July 14, 1991. The church had no doors, no carpet, no electricity, and once again, no money. I remained steadfast, unshakeable, and unmovable that the dedication would take place on the date that God had given me, and that date was July 14, 1991. I personally went to Southern Maryland Electric and shared the dilemma of the church and mentioned how embarrassing it would be for the power company if the church did not have electricity on the day of the dedication. While in the office of the power company, God sent an angel to our rescue named Mary Adams who was an employee with the power company and who would later become a member of Union Bethel. She became instrumental in expediting the process of our getting electricity. The problems did not stop there though. A company in Virginia that was to install the carpet and pews was refusing to do so because of the lack of funds. Again, after much prayer and gentle persuasion, to our surprise, the carpet and pews were delivered. The power company was working religiously to get the power turned on. Unfortunately, when the pews and carpet arrived, the church had no electricity, and we had to rent generators and drive a car up to the door to shine light into the church to give the installers light. With all that was going on, the doors and windows for the church had not arrived. Therefore, we had members of the trustee board to spend nights at the church until the doors and windows were delivered. The doors and windows arrived on July 13—the day before the dedication. On the previous Thursday, before the dedication ceremony, we had electricity. *July 13, 1991*—this is why I love to tell others that I know God is faithful and will answer prayer.

The dedication ceremonies for the new Union Bethel AME Church were held at 10:00 a.m. and 3:30 p.m. on July 14, 1991—the date God had placed on my heart. Hebrews 11:6: "And without faith it is impossible to please God, because everyone who comes to Him must believe that He exists and that He rewards those who earnestly seek Him." This captures the essence of faith that I have for God. *God is faithful!* Do not ever doubt it. I have since written a manual to assist and guide other churches with the many processes of church construction.

The manual, *More Than Bricks and Mortar: Building a Church Without Losing Your Mind*, was published in 1996.

Building a new facility was a major feat for the Brandywine congregation. It was a true test of our faith in the forever-faithful God. Today, Union Bethel AME is no longer viewed as a rural remote church, but a growing suburban church on the outskirts of our nation's capital. The church really has flourished, membership continues to increase, new ministries have been created, and community outreach services have grown by leaps and bounds. What a mighty God we serve! Since that magnificent accomplishment, the church has purchased additional land and now owns fifty-five acres of property, and we are now one church in two locations—an additional site is in Temple Hills, Maryland. As of this writing, there have been nearly fifty persons from Union Bethel AME who have accepted their calling into the ministry, including my wife, Sherita. After twenty-five years of pastoral ministry to this congregation, my wife and I continue to be excited about the work we are doing and the joy we have in serving some of the greatest people in the Christian kingdom.

Shortly after the completion of the church, things seemed to start going haywire for me. I started feeling a sense of uselessness. I believed my purpose had been fulfilled, and there was nothing left for me to do. During the construction of the church, I was driven, determined, and committed. Afterward, I began to experience what I later learned was *burnout*. I tried intercessory prayer with prayer partners, and I will forever be grateful to two United Methodist ministers, Rev. John R. Brown and Bishop C. Anthony Muse, along with minister friends from the AME churches who supported and encouraged me during this most difficult period. However, I still felt a gigantic sense of emptiness. It was at this time that I decided to enroll into the doctoral program at Howard University. By this time, Howard's School of Religion had become Howard University School of Divinity. You may be wondering what happened to my pursuit of a degree in mortuary science. When I became the pastor at Union Bethel, my involvements with the church took precedence over getting a degree in mortuary science.

Life can be bittersweet, and the playing field is not always fair. Dealing with the issues of just living life can be trying, and I do not minimize the struggles of daily living by any means. Trying to live the life of a Christian is a challenge. In my Christian walk, I have questioned God and wondered why I was given so many tests of my faith. Through the years, as I continue to grow spiritually, I have truly come to understand the power of God's grace, mercy, and love. As I reflect back, life has been good for me. God has been good and continues to be good to me.

As I continued my Christian journey, I soon realized that many times in life you don't always get what you ask for, and in many cases, you may get quite a few things you didn't ask for. I have come to learn that it is not so much of what happens to us as compared to how we react to what happens. It is not about how we begin; it is all about how we finish. I had to learn to face the music of life and, no matter what, maintain a positive attitude. Faith in God was and still is the necessary essential of my life. My tenacity to survive the worst of times has reinforced my true belief that the Lord will always make a way somehow. Don't ever forget that.

As I remember how I grew up, poor and fatherless, I now know that this condition left an indelible imprint on my life. My undeniable compassion for the needy, widows, single parents, impoverished children, and the elderly hold a gargantuan place in my life. I strive daily to make life a little better for the unfortunate that I encounter. Now, I can see more clearly how God uses difficult situations in our lives to help us see His purpose and glory. I love the hymn "Great Is Thy Faithfulness" because it reinforces that God is always faithful. More and more I need Him; therefore, I consistently stay in constant communication with Him. Through it all, God is my rock, sword, and shield.

Until around the age of thirty-eight, life for me was fairly uneventful. Despite the occasional days of drudgery, or as Bishop John Hurst Adams would say, the days of living the "human condition," I was content. I had begun work as a *fellow* with the Congress of National Black Churches Fellowship Program for Pastors at Partners for Sacred Places Inc. located in Philadelphia, Pennsylvania. I was completing my final semester of course work toward my doctor of ministry degree when I was hospitalized and diagnosed with a serious heart ailment. It was in December of 1994, while walking the streets of Philadelphia, when I began having severe chest and back pains. I was rushed to a hospital and was later told that one of my main arteries had a blockage of 90 percent. Amazingly though, I was informed that x-rays revealed that I was born with three main arteries—normally, you only have two. I was told that I was one in a million, born with three main arteries. The pressure of the blocked artery should have caused a massive heart attack, but was prevented because of the extra artery. Even though I experienced all the symptoms of a massive heart attack, there was no damage to the heart itself. Praise the Lord! To God be the glory! Great is thy faithfulness!

A month later, in January 1995, I underwent an angioplasty procedure and had a stent implanted in the blocked artery. The night before the surgery, I found solace in Psalm 30:1-6: "I will exalt you, O Lord, for you lifted me out of the depths and did not let my enemies gloat over me. O Lord my God, I called to you for help and you healed me. O Lord, you brought me up from the grave; you spared me from going down into the pit. Sing to the Lord, you saints of his; praise his holy name. For his anger lasts only a moment, but his favor lasts a lifetime; weeping may remain for a night, but rejoicing comes in the morning" (NIV Bible). The next morning (January 19, 1995), before I was rolled into surgery, I began a prayer journal, and I wrote the following entry to God:

There comes a time in life when faith in God is all that we have. Thanks to You, God, for You are the most powerful force I have. Today is the day of my angioplasty procedure. God, You are faithful. I know You are good and exact in Your ways. I pray that Your will shall be done in every form and fashion. I expect the best. I believe the best, but God, You know what is best for me. Weeping may endureth for a night, but joy comes in the morning. I sing this morning because I am happy. I sing because—Oh God—I am free. His eye is on the sparrow. I know He watches over me. I am comforted in the assurance that God, You know what is best for me. Amen.

During the surgical procedure, the angioplasty balloon pierced the artery and caused uncontrollable bleeding. After six hours, the surgeons finally stopped the bleeding. I was placed in intensive care and remained there for several days. Later, I was told that most people would not have survived the uncontrollable bleeding during heart surgery. While in intensive care, my mother, who had flown in from South Carolina, and Sherita were by my side.

What an amazing God You are! God, You and only You, gave me a second chance at life. I live to serve you. Amen. I came home from the hospital with a new determination to change my lifestyle and eating habits. Immediately I started to change my diet and began exercising as much as my healing body would allow.

During my recuperation, I began to write my doctor of ministry dissertation, "A Pastor's Role in a Church Construction Project." I found myself writing daily, working out on the treadmill, and taking short walks outdoors. This was a very humbling and yet contentious time in my life. I realized how precious life was, and that at age thirty-eight, I almost lost my life. Rather than dwell on that, I chose to glorify and give praise to God for giving me a second chance. God is a God of second chances. All you have to do is trust and believe in Him.

Prior to my surgery, there were several things that happened that helped me become stronger in my faith. In October of 1993, someone donated a box of *The One Year Bible* to Howard University's School of Divinity. This Bible was very structured and formatted for daily reading that allowed you to read the entire Bible in one year. As I began to read the Bible daily, my faith began to increase, and the joy that came to my soul and inner spirit was miraculously wonderful. I am convinced that this daily reading of the Bible was God's way of preparing me for the surgery and recuperation I would face and the task of writing a dissertation as well as other challenges that surfaced along the way.

Little did I know that God was preparing me for yet another setback of trials and tribulations. As I was recuperating, writing my doctoral ministry project, preparing to defend my work, I was anticipating graduation. Right after my defense that went well with minor changes, I ordered my cap and grown, invited family and friends to my graduation and now was excited to finally reach what seemed like a far-reaching goal.

The Thursday before graduation, I was out taking a walk and about three blocks from my house, a severe pain ripped through my chest and I started having shortness of breath. I knew something was going wrong. I was sweating and felt very tired. I stopped walking, regained my composure, and proceeded to walk a little farther. After about a half of a block, I saw a little girl sitting on the front steps of her house, and I wondered if I could make it to her so I could ask her to call 911 for me. Well as I kept walking, looking down, I looked up and I was near the house, but the girl was not there. In fact she seemed to just disappear. By this time, the pain felt better and I pressed on to my home. Once I got in the house, I took a shower, got dressed and drove myself to the Doctor's office about 10 miles (from

Clinton to Landover). Once I arrived and told the doctor of my symptoms, I was examined and rushed to Holy Cross Hospital in Silver Spring, Maryland. I was diagnosed as having another heart attack as a result of the stent implanted in January having blocked off. I was transferred to Georgetown Hospital where I underwent a second procedure to unblock the stent.

This caused me to spend the day in the intensive care, and was told that once the bleeding stopped, I would be placed in a regular room. Well, I had a major dilemma. My graduation was scheduled for Saturday and here I was on Thursday night in the ICU unit of Georgetown Hospital. I told the doctors, nurses, and everyone else who would listen about my dilemma. The bleeding continued and my hope of getting to my graduation seemed bleak. Sherita started calling family and friends, prayer chains were started, several of my close friends came to the hospital and prayed with me. The doctors and nurses were checking on me every ten minutes until the bleeding stopped.

Finally, on Friday, the doctor said to me, if you stop bleeding in one hour we will release you to attend your graduation. This was around 4:00 pm. By 5:00 pm the doctor said to me if you continue not bleeding you can go home by 6:00 pm. At 6:00 pm I was released directly from ICU to go home. I was weak but excited.

I watched the Howard University graduation by television from home and Sherita hooded me with the other students as family members watched, my mother, children, sister, her husband, and other family members from New York.

Sherita had borrowed a wheelchair from the church and she helped me to the car and drove me to Washington, DC to participate in the Divinity School graduation. There at the graduation, several things happened. I was awarded the 1995 Doctor of Ministry (D.Min.) degree and the student of the year award for outstanding dissertation. Evangelist Shirley Caesars's husband, Bishop Harold Williams was a part of my graduating class and she came over and prayed while laying hands on me. The time of the awarding of degrees, Bro. French Thompson, a member of Union Bethel pushed me to the stage in my wheelchair and I was able to walk across the stage and receive my D.Min. degree. The audience erupted in applause. I shall never forget that day of triumph and victory. I know the power of prayer is real and God answers prayers. I hung on to the prayers of people like Pastor Grainger Browning, who preached at my 39th birthday celebration; "You will March in May". I felt the prayers of people around the country, if not the world.

I had to recuperate for another six months and I stayed in the word daily. Bro. Kevin Carter, a good friend and brother was between jobs and he would pick me up in the mornings and drive me all over Maryland, discovering new places, riding boats and even fishing. The time passed quickly. Sherita remained steadfast and committed. I had to change my diet, continuously exercise, and had to relax more. The glorious part about the whole piece is that I never experienced heart damages. This is how I know when we go through different seasons in life, some good and some bad, but through it all, I am a witness that what God takes us to, He is more than able to bring us out of it.

A Prayer

April 18, 1995

Dear God, This marks an important day in my life. This is the day I will defend my dissertation for my doctor of ministry degree. God, You are in control of my life. My dissertation project is not my project; it belongs to You, God. As I begin my defense, God, I believe in Your power. I know You care. (Later that day . . .) What a powerful and blessed day. I passed my dissertation defense with a few minor corrections. The Lord has shown His faithfulness and superseded my expectations. I am so grateful, delighted, happy, proud, humbled and honored that God would bless me with a doctor of ministry degree. This is my season—my time. Love, Harry

I offer special thanks to the Reverend Drs. Lee P. Washington, Jo Ann Browning and Diana Parker for encouraging me through the doctoral writing and defense stages. Thanks to the dean, faculty, staff project team, and fellow students for their encouragement and assistance.

CHAPTER FIVE

Broken But Not to Despair Burnt Out, But Not Burnt Up

A Prayer
November 28, 1995

Dear God, It seems like most of my thoughts center around hurt and pain. I plead for your mercy and love. Frustration seems to be my lot. Lord I cry out to you. The pain is so great. The financial worries, the uncertainty of the future, Lord, please help me. I really do need your help. I submit myself to you. In Jesus Name. Amen.

IT IS AMAZING what happens when the olive is crushed and the rollers are glided over its pieces, for it is then that the anointing oil is collected. For the anointing shall break the yoke. "So he said to me, 'This is the Word of the Lord to Zerubbabel: "Not by might nor power, but by my Spirit," says the Lord Almighty'" (Zechariah 4:6). Growing up impoverished can do a major job on your psyche, particularly when you grew up in an environment where you were looked down upon and ridiculed for your living conditions, laughed at for wearing second hand clothes and clothes brought from the bargain store. My parents were hard working people and like a lot of people in the south, did what they had to do to survive. Well my parents sold liquor (unlicensed or illegal alcohol) to make ends meet.

This caused our house to be labeled as a "liquor house". This was very degrading and caused much shame and often times pain, particularly when some of my playmates were not allowed to come to my house, but I could go to theirs. This caused low self esteem and low expectations. I had to work and continue to work vigorously to overcome the spirit of poverty and shame. The results can be detrimental. Many workaholics are driven by the overwhelming fear of reliving the life of abject poverty. I speak specifically for myself right now. I am a workaholic and a frantic overachiever. Through the years, I associated work with my self-worth and the accumulation of material goods as a sign of wealth and accomplishment. By the time I had reached the age of fifty, I pretty much had everything that my heart desired. From acquiring cars and houses and traveling the world, to enjoying the finer things in life, I truly believed I had arrived. Somewhere deep from the depth of my inner soul, I genuinely loved hearing people tell me I was "all right." I worked overly hard to hear accolades from my family and friends. It was almost an obsession. I needed to hear it from Sherita, my children, my mother, siblings, coworkers, bishops, elders, colleagues, and friends, and most of all, I had to hear it from the congregations of the churches I had served as pastor. The need to serve others became self-effacing because my self-worth became wrapped up into my performance. Hearing people constantly tell you that "You're the best," "There is no one like you," "You are wonderful," "We love you," and "We need you" can be addictive to a fragile ego.

More and more I felt the need to personally fulfill all pastoral duties even when I could have delegated some responsibility to others. It was me and only me who had to visit the sick and the shut-ins. It was me who had to preach every funeral. It was me who had to perform every wedding, counsel everyone, chair every meeting, referee every fight, settle every dispute, and the list goes on and on. I believed completely that the success of

REV. DR. HARRY L. SEAWRIGHT

every church I was the pastor of rested totally with me. I will never forget the day I had a direct revelation from the Lord in which the Lord spoke to me and said, "The church is not yours . . . I am in charge, not you." This was revealed to me after much confusion, discouragement, and exhaustion with trying to lead God's people. With God speaking to me, I began to pray daily for more understanding of the realization that the church or churches in which I was the pastor did not belong to me; the church belonged to God. As a pastor, you would think I would have known this, but my need for recognition overshadowed God's need for me.

Realizing that God is in charge helped me tremendously in alleviating my need to be a "people pleaser." I began to rely more and more on His Word, and one scripture in particular helped me to reach this milestone: "Why fear people who can destroy the body, but not the soul" (Matthew 10:28). Today, I look back in wonder, and I find it unbelievable that my obsession to please people and not God led to failing health, broken relationships, a state of exhaustion, and almost destroyed my marriage and family. My need to please people caused me to seek affirmation and confirmation from all the wrong sources. I finally realized, through divine intervention, that I was called by God and He is the one to whom I report, not man. God is the one who holds us accountable for all our actions and deeds. He is the one and only one who is able to wipe our slates clean and make us brand-new. Therefore, as long as we get it right with God, everything else will fall into place. I don't have to please man, just God. And I am on a renewed mission to do just that. I am alive today to do God's will.

The more I seek God, the more I find time to spend with Him in prayer and in the reading of His Word. In order to get to know Him, you must spend time with Him. Matthew 6:33 tells us to "seek first the Kingdom of God and all of His righteousness and all other things would be added unto you." Through living this scripture, my life has been transformed. The transformation is real. God is real, and He lives in my soul. When I look back over my life, my soul cries out in wonder because it was God and only Him who got me over.

I have repeatedly apologized to God for learning the hard way that He does not want us wandering aimlessly, pleasing people, and overworking ourselves to the point of being overwhelmed, exhausted, and driven to a state of illness. God loves us and cares for us too much to see us live a life inundated with insurmountable burdens and pains. I had to do a great deal of work to break the chains of obsessing to pleasing people. God only wants us to do our best according to His Word. He wants us to do our best each and every day. We should never be too busy for God. He is never too busy for us. As a pastor, the one thing that has become the capstone and foundation for me, which has also helped me to get through periods of being burnt out in my life, was to become totally dependent on God. I have emerged and have learned the art of taking care of one's self by developing healthy eating habits, learning the necessity of physical exercise, following weight management, finding quality family time, becoming involved with support groups and, most of all, making "me time" with God . . . where I just rest in His spirit. It is truly amazing what can happen when you spend time with God.

Through it all, I am undoubtedly a better and more profound Christian due to my transformation. I am full of life, more vibrant, and I have learned to listen and discern the voice of God. My personal success rate has risen to new heights. Reaching this plateau was not easy and only occurred after I began to set boundaries and began to focus on my body as a temple of God. Furthermore, I had to thoroughly look at my value system; I had to learn how to trust others and delegate more responsibility to others. Slowly my circle of assistants began to grow, and my life took on a new purpose. As my understanding of who I am in

God continued to emerge, life had more meaning, and I became a better leader. I credit much of this to spending invaluable time with God. During this ordeal, my marriage had suffered as well. My wife and I sought marriage counseling, and with God's help, our marriage became the rock and foundation for our existence. I began to let go and let God. I joined a pastoral support group and faithfully attended and eagerly participated in the sessions. When you allow burdens to weigh you down, it is difficult for you to see the forest because you are too busy looking at the trees. Letting go and letting God direct your footsteps will allow you to see what He has for you. Philippians 4:13 stands as a true reminder that "I can do all things through Christ who strengthens me."

As a result of the new changes in my life, revelations and visions began to surface not only on a personal level but also on a professional level. Union Bethel was able to purchase additional land for expansion, the membership of the church began to grow by leaps and bounds, new ministries in the church were birthed, and the church coffers increased favorably. My lifelong desire to own a business came into fruition. Within a five-year period, I found myself at the helm of twelve different business ventures with almost one hundred employees.

In the midst of all the missteps that I made on my ministerial journey, today I can fervently say that God is able and willing to supply us with our needs when we need it if we are willing to follow His lead. God is not going to neglect us nor will He forsake us. His love for us is the greatest love of all. Can you imagine giving your only begotten son as a sacrifice in order that others may have eternal life? As I digress for a moment and reflect to 1994 and 1995, when I was on the brink of death after having major heart disease and heart procedures to repair the damage done to my arteries, I can't help but remember that in May of 1995, through the miraculous power of God, one day after being released from intensive care at Georgetown University

Hospital, I received my doctor of ministry degree from Howard University School of Divinity. Even though I received my degree in a wheelchair, it was through God's grace that I received it. I am constantly reminded of how good God really is when I see someone who is in a wheelchair. Because you see, it could be worse.

As I was going through the many challenges of life as a pastor, a group of ministers in the area had formed a clergy support group about a year earlier. When they heard about my plight, I was invited to join the group. After all I had encountered, I did not hesitate. I knew God had sent them as a vessel to offer me support. Union Bethel AME was going through some major changes. Several members of my ministerial staff and their families had left the ministry, and more and more responsibility was falling on my shoulders during a time when I thought I was able to let some things go. Because of health reasons, I was unsure about my career, my continued ministry at Union Bethel, and even my faith in God was questionable. My marriage was falling apart, and it looked as if I was headed for a divorce. My personal finances were another issue that weighed me down. After two heart attacks within four months of each other, my doctors were advising me not to continue in the ministry. They believed it was too much for my fragile arteries. Little did they know that I knew another doctor, and that doctor is Jesus. He is the ultimate healer.

As I began to find my way, the support group welcomed me, listened to me, offered advice, loved, and accepted me. Before I knew it, the pieces to the puzzle of my life began to fit. Sherita and I went to marriage counseling, my book was published in 1996, and I started my first business, HLS Consulting Inc.—a company specializing in church construction, administration, and finance. Union Bethel AME established its first outreach center, and Bethel House, a 501(c)(3), was opened, rendering assistance to the less fortunate by providing educational training and other support to those in need. A couple of years later in 1998, Union Bethel purchased twenty-one acres of land adjacent to the church. Two years later, we purchased an additional ten acres, and a few years later, we obtained an additional fifteen acres. With the accumulation of more property, the church was able to organize and provide summer camp, and we opened a before-and after-school care center. You see what happens when you let go and let God. Hence, God was not finished blessing us.

Two children in our before-and after-school program moved to the Temple Hills, Maryland, area and were falling behind in their studies. As a church family, we began to seek out ways we could continue to support them. God led us to the Temple Hills area to explore the possibility of opening an educational center there, and to our amazement, we were led to an old Rite Aid drugstore that was no longer being used. The owners offered us several amenities to lease the building, and there we found an opportunity we could not refuse. As a result, we organized another 501(c)(3) and opened another before-and after-school facility housing a kindergarten and a day care for infants to four-year-olds. We also used the 14,000-square-foot building for banquet operations on Friday, Saturday, and Sunday afternoons. In addition to using the facility as a school and a banquet hall, we began having Sunday morning worship services there and Bible study and other midweek activities. Before long, Union Bethel AME was operating as one church in two locations. Just a few years later, Unity Economic Development Corporation, another 501(c)(3), was created as an avenue to build a community center on a portion of property in Brandywine, Maryland. Today, this nonprofit operates a certified HUD (Housing and Urban Development) counseling program that offers foreclosure prevention and home-buyers education.

At one point, I served as the president or chairman of the board of each 501(c)(3). The opportunities continued to come to me personally as well. In 2002, with the support of my wife, Sherita; the assistance of a good friend, Melvin Greene, who was a college roommate at Benedict College and is the accountant for my business enterprises; and another wonderful friend, Attorney Midget Parker, my second business venture—*We Kleen Inc.*, a cleaning company, was created. Within six months of starting the company, I was able to hire my first employees to begin cleaning homes. Shortly thereafter, God blessed me with a commercial contract, and within a few years, I had twenty-five employees, and the business was steadily growing and continues to grow. Out of the creation of the cleaning business, other opportunities abounded. A handyman service and a landscaping service were created under the umbrella of *We Kleen Inc.* I have since sold 40 percent of the company to E. Connell Alexander, who is a faithful prayer partner. God was truly blessing me, and to Him I continue to give the glory. God will give us the desires of our heart if we are faithful to Him.

You see, God was not finished with me yet. The next business opportunity came after purchasing a house to serve as office space for the cleaning company. With God's guidance, my wife and I began investing in properties, and this concept materialized into a property management business, *Prestigious Property Management Inc.* While managing all my business ventures, I served as treasurer of the Second Episcopal District of the AME Church, the Washington Conference, and the Religious, Charitable, and Educational Board of the Second Episcopal District (RED Inc.). It was astonishing to me, just a few years before, how I was questioning how a degree in business administration was going to enhance me as a minister. God provided the answers to my questions, and He has allowed me, with my degree in business administration, to provide much-needed assistance to many other churches in preparing their financial statements, getting loans from banks, and building and financing church construction projects.

God does not want us to waste our gifts, and He will provide us opportunity after opportunity to utilize our God-given talents. As individuals, we need to use our natural gifts and talents to advance the Kingdom of God. I encourage seminaries to offer business-related courses for aspiring ministers and pastors. The church is a business, and those at the helm of a church need to know the intricate details of operating the church as a business while saving souls. I am forever grateful to God for allowing me to look into a Benedict College yearbook and see a picture of someone from my nearby hometown that had majored in business administration, and at that moment, the light bulb came on for me. Through the years, I have taught workshops to help others start their own businesses. I have been an investor with helping others realize their dreams of owning a business from a men's clothing store to a meat manufacturing company. "God works in mysterious ways, His wonders to perform. He plants His footsteps on the sea, and rides upon the storm." God did it for me, and He can do it for you too.

Many of you can probably see how I reached the level of being burnt out. However, as stated in the title of this chapter, I was not burnt up because God saw to it. In fact, in 1992, Bishop H. Hartford Brookins invited me to preach the annual sermon at the forty-second session of the Washington Conference, and the title of my sermon was "Burnt Out, but Not Burnt Up." The scripture for the sermon came from Jeremiah 20. You see, Jeremiah, after being beaten and humiliated publicly, had become frustrated with the ministry. And in verse 9, he says, "I will not mention Him or speak any more in His name, His word is in my heart like a fire, a fire shut up in my bones. I am weary of holding it in; indeed, I cannot." Almost twenty years later, I have persons who were witnesses to that sermon say that it was one of the most memorable sermons preached at an annual conference. After that sermon, I sought professional counseling and continued to garner help from the ministerial support group.

God, I thank you for my brothers of the cloth: Bishop Robert Prichett, Reverends Dr. Lee P. Washington, Michael Turner, Robert Hodges, and the late Dr. Norris Sydnor. I am grateful to their wives Elder Christine Prichett, Ann Washington, Rev. Eunice Turner, Delores Hodges and Queen Sydnor. These women embraced Sherita as a sister and me as a brother. We are better because of them. These Christian brothers allowed me to vent and encouraged me to dream and live my dreams. Without hesitation, they also voiced their concerns and opinions, all in the spirit of love, when I needed to hear a voice of reason and even scorn. I will forever be grateful for their genuine support. There were so many others who provided numerous prayers for Sherita and me, especially during the times of my heart attacks. As the saying goes, "When prayers go up, blessings come down." During one episode, when I was laying in my hospital bed, I actually felt the divine power of those praying for me. I experienced a sensation as if I were actually floating on the bed. I knew I was being lifted by prayer. Once again, as I look back over my life, I know God will place people in your life at critical times when you need them the most.

As God continues to bless me and repair me, I offer myself to others who may be experiencing or have experienced some of the same things I encountered. There were many times I asked God why was I going through what I was going through, but now I thank Him for my troubles as well as my blessings. Setbacks are setups for a comeback if you believe and trust in God. He is not going to let you fail. God had to help me define who I was to Him. It took a lot of retrospection, introspection, and redirection of my life. He took me out of me and replaced the me with more of Him. God taught me the value of life and how to truly live a life dedicated to Him. Through it all, I have learned to trust in Jesus; I have learned to trust in God.

A Prayer

December 24, 2007

Dear God, How wonderful You are! How blessed I am to have a Savior like You. I am so grateful for Your Son, Jesus. I am so grateful during this holiday season for Your love and mercy. My family is well, and You continue to bless me abundantly. My business, *We Kleen*, is doing okay. Union Bethel has had some challenges, but we are holding on because You are faithful. I really do love You, Lord. I am putting all my trust in You. Continue to strengthen my life, my home, my marriage, my children, my grandson, and my friends. Thank you, Lord, and I do love You. Amen.

CHAPTER SIX

Something Divine Within:
The Role of the Pastor

Something Within

"Preachers and teachers would make their appeal, fighting as soldiers on great battlefields; when to their pleadings my poor heart did yield, all I could say, there is something within." (Written by Lucie E. Campbell)

A S MY LIFE took on a new focus and meaning, the old me disappeared, and a new me began to emerge. My energy was being spent more and more on my role as a pastor. In doing so, I had to take another look at every one of my assumptions and values from the past. Once again, I had to go deep within myself to a place I had not gone before. God had been too good to me for me to hold on to fear, anger, guilt, and pain. I was determined to see things differently, and by seeing things differently, I found my defining role as a pastor.

In the general tradition of the church, a pastor is someone who leads, proclaims the gospel, and cares for the people within a congregation. A pastor should be able to relate well with people in ways that are personal, caring, and compassionate and, which in turn, evoke feelings of trust, comfort, and respect for people. In leading, proclaiming, and caring, pastors have many functions. They are called upon to be visionary leaders, good administrators, outstanding fund-raisers, counselors, teachers, community activists, and friends. The list can become endless because many people see their pastor in different perspectives and roles. In every church in which I served as pastor, my role was somewhat slightly different in each congregation.

Because pastors have so many roles and expectations to fulfill, it is not difficult for pastors to reach a state of *burnout* as I did. There have been many scholarly books written regarding the role of the pastor. However, until you have walked the walk and talked the talk, it is extremely difficult to relate. As a pastor since the age of twenty-one, I can truly say that I had to learn how to relate to the demands and expectations of others. Many times I sacrificed family time and personal "me" time to come to the aid of a congregant. When members of my church came to me seeking assistance, whether it was the birth of a baby, a death, a wedding, a baptism, a surgery, a hospitalization, an incarceration, and even a birthday celebration, I was there. I have been called upon to intervene in family feuds and to serve as a character witness in child custody hearings and divorce cases. As a pastor, I had been multitasking before the phrase became fashionable. Our role, as stated previously, is endless and forever evolving. Pastors might find themselves leaving a funeral in haste to go and perform at a wedding ceremony or perform a baby dedication or a baptismal after receiving a call or text message that a faithful parishioner is dying and that the family is in need of you immediately.

After all that I had experienced as a pastor and after the "trials and tribulations," I came to a place at Union Bethel AME where I could see that my role was to proclaim, lead, and care. The three—proclaim, lead, and care—must work together as one with each being dependent upon the other and each having equal prominence and importance.

Most church members on the average see their pastor as someone who is to lead the congregation spiritually through bringing the Word regularly to them. Week after week the pastor is expected to deliver an inspiring message that will leave an indelible mark on his/her worshipers. This is a given and clearly the most important role of the pastor—*being able to proclaim the Word.*

However, there are people who come to church to try and make sense of their everyday existence. Pastors fulfill this need by proclaiming biblical stories and making them relevant to the parishioners' lives. In *Sacrifice and Delight,* Alan Jones says that the task of any pastor is to tell stories, perform rituals, and act as a lightning rod for the issues and anxieties of the day. He goes on to say that pastors are ordained to bring people to threshold experiences where they can understand life afresh. Those of us who are pastors must come to the realization, if we have not already, that the importance of proclamation can never be underestimated. I know of no other institution, besides the church, where people will come to hear the same person proclaim a message day after day and week after week for many years. I just recently celebrated twenty-five years of being the pastor at Union Bethel AME. For twenty-five years, in our complex and ever-changing world, God has given me the spiritual know-how to proclaim proper spiritual direction to guide the congregation to function to its highest capacity. Proclaiming God's Word is awesome!

Not only is it necessary for the pastor to proclaim God's Word to the congregation; the pastor must be a visionary leader for the congregation. A successful pastor should be able to present ideas while addressing the needs of those members who seek his or her advice and guidance in all aspects of the life and work of the congregation. It is the pastor's duty to assist the members with carrying out the defined mission statement of the church. The mission should not be confused with the church's vision. The mission statement of the church is a broad, general statement about where the church wishes to reach and what the church hopes to accomplish. On the other hand, the vision is a more concrete and sustainable idea that acts as an instrument to allow the mission to happen. The pastor must know the difference between the two and must be able to carry out the mission as well as serve as a leader who can initiate and implement new ideas. Through the years, I have had many visionary pastors to befriend me, and I am a true believer that pastors who actively seek to fulfill God's vision for their ministry are a treasure to their congregations. It is through divine leadership that they have been able to blend their vision for personal ministry with the vision imparted by God for the churches they lead. One must have an accurate understanding of God, self, and circumstances in order to lead. Over the years, as a pastor, I have often referred to Proverbs 29:18, "Where there is no vision, the people perish."

Leadership skills are essential to the success of a pastor. Leadership can carry a pastor from the pulpit on Sunday and out into the community streets on Monday. It was the great civil rights leader, Dr. Martin Luther King Jr., who proclaimed that "one cannot lead where he does not go." It is my belief that pastoral leadership is expressed best by proclaiming God's Word through His teachings to us. He wants pastors to lead His people according to His Word. Because, you see, God's Word will never fail.

As important as proclaiming God's Word and leading God's people according to His Word is, pastors must be caring and compassionate. Whether our congregations are small or whether we are the pastor of a megachurch, people with a myriad of wants and concerns will need us. The pastor is expected to be at their beck and call. Pastors are to be enablers and encouragers, helping others identify and respond to their needs. One of the problems I continue to face as a pastor is not being as easily accessible to my congregation as I was maybe five years ago. Those members who were accustomed to stopping by the church at any time of the day, coming into my office without an appointment, and sitting and talking for several hours are livid at having to make an appointment to see me. It does not mean that I no longer care about my members. A part of caring is being able to find a balance between pastoral duties and your personal needs. You will never be able to successfully help others through life's situations if you do not find the time to take care of yourself. Also, as a pastor, one of our many functions is to tell others in a caring, nonjudgmental way when they are not following the precepts of God's Word. As I continue to proclaim God's Word, serve as a leader, and exalt care and compassion for the people of God at Union Bethel AME and throughout the world, Jeremiah 3:15 serves as a reminder that God continues to do a mighty work in my life: "And I will give you pastors according to my heart, which shall feed you with knowledge and understanding." I will continue to say it until I cannot say it anymore: God is a good and faithful God.

REV. DR. HARRY L. SEAWRIGHT

A Prayer

January 4, 1996

Dear God, Thank you so much for your blessings. Thank you for all the activities of this day and the past days. I feel the power of your blessings. I thank you for allowing my business to get off the ground. God, I love you for your Grace and Mercy. Please continue to look beyond my faults and see my needs. Bless Union Bethel. Thank you for being my personal friend and my everlasting partner. In Jesus Name. Amen.

Typical Daily Schedule

5:45 a.m.	Wake-up call, prayer, and selection of scripture for Prayer Line
	Notes:
6:00 a.m.	Dial International Prayer Line
	Notes:
6:30 a.m.	Devotions, prayer, Bible and devotional material reading
	Notes:
7:30 a.m.	
	Notes:
7:45 a.m.	Family prayer
	Notes:
8:00 a.m.	Exercise
	Notes:
8:45 a.m.	Breakfast (Take medications)
	Notes:
10:00 a.m.-noon	Appointments: - -
	Notes:
Noon-1:00 p.m.	Lunch

REV. DR. HARRY L. SEAWRIGHT

	Appointments:
2:00-4:00 p.m.	-
	-
	Notes:
5:30 p.m.	Dinner
6:30 p.m.	Rest, Nap
7:30 p.m.	Meetings
	Notes:
10:00 p.m.	Prayer/Bedtime

Typical Weekly Schedule						

Sunday	Monday	Tuesday	Wednesday	Thursday	Friday	Saturday
7:45 a.m. Worship at Brandywine *10:00 a.m.* Worship at Temple Hills *11:00 a.m.* *Worship at Brandywine *4:00 p.m.* Afternoon Service or Preaching -Away from Union Bethel	Day off from work	Meetings/ Office	7:30 p.m. Bible Study	10:00 a.m. Support Group	Service Preparation and Family Time	As Needed

---

*   I go to the Temple Hills site once a month to preach or give pastoral remarks.

     REV. DR. HARRY L. SEAWRIGHT

CHAPTER SEVEN

Facing the Challenges
of Tremendous Loss

A Prayer
November 19, 2005

Dear God, I did not know that life could send so much pain. My heart is aching, and I have never experienced pain like I am experiencing right now. The death of my mother has caused me to hurt in places of my heart I did not know existed. My God, You are my helper, shield, and buckler. I hold on to You, Jesus, the Holy Spirit, praying for guidance and strength. I am trusting and believing in You, for I know You are the only one that can fix it for me. Thanks for Sherita, my sisters and brothers, children, other family members, the Union Bethel family, as well as the multitude of friends who are praying for me. Thanks for all Your love. Harry.

THIS DAY WILL be forever imprinted in my mind. For this day I went to the bedside and saw the lifeless body of my dear mother. My mother was an invaluable part of my life since the passing of my father when I was five years of age. She was a strong woman, strong-willed and determined in every way. She was a survivor and was forever trying to make things happen for her family. I saw her face the challenges of life with much prayer, faith, and hard work. She epitomized what the book of James called "faith without works is dead" (James 2:17). With her ninth grade education, she was one gifted and talented woman, and I thank God I had the privilege of having her as my mother. She endured the pains of life, faced the music with a dance, kept smiling, and was so kind in spirit, heart, and mind.

My mother was a domestic worker who shared her talents of cooking and cleaning while rearing her children as well as the children of the people for whom she worked. She took in two of her sisters after their mother passed, Bernice Edmond and Connie Fields Corley (deceased). She allowed her sister's children and my father's nieces and nephews to stay at our house during the summer, raised her three grandchildren, Barbara Lynn, Lance and Eric, when their mother, Emma Ruth, passed. She started and managed several businesses (i.e., a nightclub, a store, a barbecue stand, managed a softball team, kept a garden, raised chickens, pigs, kept goats, and any stray dogs and cats that came around the house). Wonder how I got my entrepreneurial spirit? At one point in her life, she went to New York on a sleep-in job to earn money to care for her children. She purchased property and had a home built. She became a day-care provider for several of her grandchildren. She was a member and regularly attended her church, Prodigal African Methodist Episcopal Church of Swansea, South Carolina. My mom was an active choir member who also served the church as a stewardess, class leader, and member of the Pastor's Aid Club, and she was an ordained deaconess. She was an Eastern Star and a member of the Women's Home Christian Union.

My mother could not drive, but always owned a car and taught many of her children and grandchildren how to drive. I will never forget at age thirteen, she told me to get in the car and drive. I turned the key; the car started. She said, "Now put it in reverse, back out, then put it in drive and move forward. Keep turning the wheel and go straight." I was all over the road because I kept turning the wheel back and forth. Fortunately, there were no other cars on the road. That episode began my trek of learning how to drive. My sisters and brothers started giving me opportunities to drive. Two years later, I had my learner's permit and was driving my mother all over the place.

During those days of driving her here and there, we really became close. She would give her wise counsel, guidance, and advice. She would repeat her favorite sayings: "Nothing beats a failure, but a try"; "Manners will take you where money will never reach you"; "Always pray to God, and He will make a way"; "Keep the faith"; "Always say thank you when someone does something for you"; "Stay in church"; "Save enough money to always be able to come back home if you need to do so." She always reminded me until she could not say it anymore of how much she was praying for me. God, you know, there isn't anything like a praying mother.

When I left South Carolina as previously stated, my mother was in my corner, encouraging me and praying for me. We talked at least two or three times a week and always kept each other abreast of the happenings in our lives and what was going on in the lives of other family members. She was so happy when Sherita and I were married because she felt I would be all right with a wife to share my life and "keep my back." She quickly reminded Sherita that even though she was my wife, she was the mother. Sherita took it in stride and treated her with utmost respect and love. Sherita would make it a point to always take her shopping for a new dress, hat, and accessories when she visited us. She would travel to Washington, DC, and Maryland by car, train, airplane, or bus. She came for the birth of our children. Mother came when I preached the annual sermon at the Washington Conference in April 1992. She came when I had my first angioplasty procedure in January 1995. She came for my graduation from Howard University School of Religion in May 1981. (My entire immediate family came from Swansea,

South Carolina and Philadelphia, Pennsylvania when I received my master of divinity degree from Howard University in May 1981.) She came for my graduation in May 1995 when I received my doctor of ministry degree from Howard University School of Divinity. My mother was always there for all major events in my life.

When Alzheimer's disease consumed my mother's body and she became incapacitated, it was a devastating blow to me and my family. By this time, two of my siblings had passed away: Emma Ruth (1979) and Dorothy (1998). However, my remaining siblings, Louise, Joseph, Ernest, Eugene, and I banded together, making sure she was cared for properly. Louise and her husband owned a community care facility for the elderly, and they were able to take Mother in as a client. During this time, I made frequent trips to South Carolina and assisted with much of her living and medical expenses. My sister, Louise, and I became her legal guardians by power of attorney and made sure her business affairs stayed in order. Closing up her house and relocating her to my sister's facility was not an easy task. She first saw us as her enemies, and it was tough goings at times. However, with much prayer, faith, and determination, it all worked out.

Monday morning, November 14, 2005, started out as a regular, routine day for me. I was out taking care of some business when Sherita called me on my cell phone to say that my sister, Louise, called to tell me that the doctor had given up on my mother and I needed to get home to South Carolina as soon as possible. Sherita made airline reservations, and I left for South Carolina that evening, arriving in Swansea around 10:30 p.m. When I arrived, my mother was unconscious, but opened her eyes and looked at me. I believe she recognized that I was there. I stayed at her bedside for the next several days, sleeping in the chair by her bed at night and keeping vigil during the day. By Friday evening, she seemed to be improving. My family and I began to cling to hope and were trying to believe in the possibilities of God. We held on to whatever hope we could. Many family members and friends of the family were coming by. Much prayer was going forth, and we, the family, decided we would trust God no matter what the outcome would bring. Earlier that week, after seeing her condition, I released her to God and even told her so. Hospice care was there, and they were very attentive, not only to her but also to us. After it appeared as if she was improving, the hospice nurse advised me to go to my place, which was next door, and get some rest, and she assured me that she would be there with my mother throughout the night. I said my good-byes and went next door to the place where I was staying.

Saturday morning at 6:10 a.m. my brother-in-law, Junior, called to inform me that Mother had passed. At that moment, I did what I felt a minister would do. After I got dressed, I went next door, gathered the family and friends who were coming from what seemed like all directions, and had prayer. I accepted God's will and thanked God for giving her eighty-six years of life, my forty-nine years of having a mother, and thanked God for her legacy. However, when the mortician came to remove her body and walked out of that room with her lifeless body in a bag, I felt that my whole world had fallen apart. That day, by far, had been one of the darkest days of my life. I went back to where I was staying, and I heard a voice asking me, "Are you going to read your Bible today as you usually do?" I had been reading my Bible every day without failure since October 1993. I had only missed reading it the two times when I was in intensive care for the heart procedures. But I told myself that if ever I needed the Word of God, it was this day. I prayed to God, Jesus, and the Holy Spirit for strength and read my *One Year Bible* for that day. I felt so much better and was able to start the new journey in my life without my mother. I have not missed a day of reading the Word of God from my *One Year Bible.*

My family and I made the necessary funeral arrangements. I asked the family if I could preach at her funeral, and they all consented. We planned the program, selected the casket and flowers, and did all the things that needed to be done. Sherita drove down with Cameron (our grandson). Matthew took a plane and Shari arrived the day of the funeral. The Union Bethel Church family came on a chartered bus while several people drove. Several of my close friends and many fellow clergy, ministerial staff, and administrative staff members came. Other friends arrived from other parts of the country. Family members came from near and far. I will never forget when I walked out of the doors of the church after the funeral. Standing at the bottom of the steps were several of my high school classmates with outstretched arms. Oh, the ministry of presence! I shall never forget the feelings I experienced as a result of the love and care of people at that dark time in my life.

My mother ended up having one of the largest funerals to ever be held at Prodigal AME Church. After thinking about the turnout and kindness from so many people, I am forever grateful that she touched so many people and taught us how to love and share with people. She truly fed the hungry and was an encourager to so many people. No matter how many times she saw people, she greeted them as if she had not seen them in a long time.

It was after the funeral and when everyone had gone back home and I had returned to Maryland, when the real mourning started for me. There were times I felt so overwhelmed, burdened down, and hurt that I thought I was losing my mind. I went to counseling to talk about my feelings. For the first time, I began to reexamine all the things I said to other people during their time of sorrow. The counseling did help my grieving. However, my grief was further complicated because before the loss of my mother, several other significant people in my life had passed away. My former administrative assistant at Hemingway Temple,

Brother Henry Washington, passed in September 2005, and the former chairman of the Steward Board also at Hemingway Temple, Brother John Cox Sr., passed away in October. Dr. Joseph C. McKinney, my mentor, had passed a month earlier. My godmother, Sister Glendora Sledge of Payne Memorial, passed a month after my mother. And Sister Ida Lipscombe, the wife of the Rev. Dr. Leon G. Lipscombe, passed; she was a wonderful encourager and a true friend. Another godmother and a good friend of my mother, Sister Mary Jane Salvage, passed away in September of the same year. I participated in all those funerals, preaching the eulogy for my mother and my two godmothers.

By the beginning of 2006, I was a basket case. I continued to pray. With the support of Sherita, my children, sisters and brother, grandchild, friends, support group, the Union Bethel Church family, and God's mercy and grace, I made it. It was so difficult ministering to others while I was hurting myself. But I have learned that God's grace is sufficient for every trial we face. I understand what the gospel artist Marvin Sapp means when he sings, "Never would have made it, without You, I would have lost it all, but now I can see that You were there for me." I have also learned that God will grow you in the midst of your pain and suffering. I have become a better student of God. I look at grieving differently now. I am no longer quick to offer people quick words to their grief.

My wife wrote a book entitled *When Momma Died* (2001). Even though she had written the book after her mother passed in March 1991, I could not read it until my mother passed. It really helped me understand better the grieving process and how to deal with my feelings. God is good, and today, I often think of my mother. I cannot think of a day I have not thought of her in some way. I think about her and remember her wit, wisdom, and often funny things she did or said. I see her spirit alive in my children and grandchild as well as her other grandchildren and great-grandchildren. She lives on in our hearts, and I will never forget the smile and peace on her face the morning she went home to be with the Lord. I will forever be grateful to God for giving me two powerful and wonderful parents, Joe Nathan and Mary Leatha Seawright. May you both rest in peace.

When I think of my mother, I think of the poem written by Langston Hughes, *Mother to Son:*

REV. DR. HARRY L. SEAWRIGHT

Mother to Son

Well, son, I'll tell you:
Life for me ain't been no crystal stair.
It's had tacks in it,
And splinters,
And boards torn up,
And places with no carpet on the floor—
Bare.
But all the time
I'se been a-climbin' on,
And reachin' landin's,
And turnin' corners,
And sometimes goin' in the dark
Where there ain't been no light.
So boy, don't you turn back.
Don't you set down on the steps
'Cause you finds it's kinder hard.
Don't you fall now—
For I'se still goin', honey,
I'se still climbin',
And life for me ain't been no crystal stair.

CHAPTER EIGHT

Listening to God, Obeying His Call

A Prayer
June 12, 2006

Dear God, Today is Pentecost Sunday, and I am so grateful for Your precious gift of the Holy Spirit. I am so grateful to my Savior, Jesus Christ, who is our wonderful helper in time of need, teacher, and a trusted friend indeed. Today feels a little strange. God, I know You are leading and guiding me to higher heights. I want to be in Your perfect will and do the right thing. Please lead me, guide me to go in the way You want me to go. I am weak, but You are strong. Thanks again for all You do for me. Love, Harry

"**WHO CAN KNOW the mind of God? His ways are so far from our ways" (Isaiah 55:8-13)**. For six weeks, I had been prompted by the Holy Spirit between 4:00 and 5:00 a.m. to get up and pray. I would lie before God, asking Him each morning to show me what He wanted me to do. At this time in my life, things were going quite well. The family was doing well. With the help of counseling, I was adjusting to my mother's death that had occurred eight months earlier. I was enjoying my marriage, children, and my three-year–old grandson, Cameron. My businesses were doing well. Union

Bethel had started a capital stewardship campaign that was well on its way of paying off the church's debt. By this time, I had just turned fifty and was feeling as if I had accomplished many of my life's goals. My goal was to retire from the pastoral ministry by age fifty-five and concentrate on my consulting company, which I established in 1995, *HLS Consulting Inc.,* a company specializing in assisting others with developing leadership and management skills on how to finance church construction projects. The company was formed as a result of my book, *More Than Bricks and Mortar: Building a Church Without Losing Your Mind.* I had purchased several investment properties and invested into twelve different enterprises including what the church owned and operated: an outreach center, day care, kindergarten, before-and after-school care school, summer camp, banquet hall, and an economic development corporation. I had my plans, but as Christians know, God has a way of overriding our wishes, wants, and desires if it is not a part of His plans for us. I have learned that His plans are far greater than any plan of my own.

One of the things that always lingered in my head was my medical condition. I often wondered about my longevity. I was living in fear because of my previous diagnosis of heart disease. In January 2005, I was admitted to the hospital after thinking that I was experiencing symptoms of another heart attack. After a three-day stay and several tests, the doctor reported to me that my heart was in perfect condition. It was the tenth anniversary of having had an angioplasty procedure after two heart attacks. This news gave me great confidence and reassurance that I could continue to pursue and fulfill my dreams. After continuous prayer, I kept hearing God say "more." I asked repeatedly, "God, what do you want me to do?" On Pentecost Sunday in June of 2006, I awakened as usual at 5:45 a.m., prayed, read my devotional materials and the daily scriptures from the *One Year Bible.* During my devotional reading that morning, I began to read 1 Timothy 3:1, "And this is a true saying, He who desires the office of a bishop desires a good work." This scripture really, really resonated with me. Not only had others predicted that I would preach one day, I had several prophecies that one day I would be a bishop. I vividly remember, six months after preaching my initial sermon, I was the guest pastor for a youth day service at an African Methodist Episcopal Church in Orangeburg, South Carolina, when an older gentleman jumped from his seat and ran across the church, shouting out and pointing at me saying, "You are going to be a bishop." He kept repeating it several times. At that time in my life, I hardly knew anything about what was involved in being a bishop.

Ministry was relatively new to me, and I did not have any personal knowledge of its depth. A cousin, the late Elise Earle Walker, who had been my fifth grade teacher, was married to a Baptist minister, Reverend Alfonso Walker. He participated, along with Sherita's father, in performing our wedding ceremony.

My association with pastors had been very limited even though my mother's grandfather, Reverend Moses Butler, was an AME pastor. He provided the land and helped organize a church in Orangeburg, South Carolina. Because of this, the church was named in his honor. Butler Chapel AME continues to be a viable and active church today even though a few years ago it was vandalized and burned to the ground. It was one of the churches in the South that succumbed to a rash of racially motivated church burnings. The congregation has rebuilt at another location. Surprisingly, after I became a minister, I found out that my father's grandfather, Reverend J. D. Lykes, had also been an AME minister who later became a presiding elder. My pastor, Reverend John Lee Davis, was fairly new to my home church; and the previous pastor, Reverend Isaiah Felder, who had been at Prodigal AME for seventeen years, was the one who I grew up under. I did not get a chance to become closely associated with him. Although people of the cloth were all around me, it was not until I was a student at Benedict College and became involved with the Gordon-Jenkins Pre-Theological Association that I began to explore the basic foundations of the ministry. This organization provided me with a platform to pray and speak in public—something I had never done before. After about six years into the ministry, my oldest brother, Joseph, obeyed God's call on his life and became an AME pastor. The African Methodist Episcopal Church has been a trademark in my life as long as I can remember.

On Pentecost Sunday 2006, I preached a sermon that day about the "Inward Filling of the Holy Spirit." The service that day was a blessing from the Lord. He truly was doing great things in my life. The Holy Spirit was telling me to seek the office of bishop of the African Methodist Episcopal Church. I had not shared this vision with anyone, not even Sherita. After service that day, my wife, and children went to dinner; we were joined by the Reverend Reginald Crump (a son in the ministry who had grown up in Union Bethel AME), and the Reverend Derrick Brown, another son in ministry. During dinner, my wife and the Reverends Crump and Brown stated that they needed to talk with me. Immediately my thoughts went to the church, and I asked them, "What is wrong now?" They said to me that they felt in their spirit that I needed to consider running to become bishop. My mouth flew open, and I began to laugh. "My God, how did they know?" I told them that I had been asking God to show me a sign and direct my path as to what He wanted me to do next.

That moment sealed my candidacy for bishop. After speaking with my bishop, the Right Reverend Adam J. Richardson, Jr.; my presiding elder, Reverend Dr. Goodwin Douglas; my immediate family; Union Bethel; and support group and other trusted friends, the campaign began. Sister Pamela King-Williams, a talented, gifted, creative, and energetic member of Union Bethel and the director of public relations for the church, became my campaign administrator.

People began volunteering, and donations started coming in from around the world. The campaign became a notable success, and we were well on our way to St. Louis, Missouri, for the Forty-Eighth Session of the General Conference where the new bishop would be elected. Before the election, I knew I was the underdog and that it would take a miracle from God for me to win. Therefore, when the first ballot was cast and I did not receive enough votes to remain in the race, I accepted it with the attitude that I had given it my best and this was not God's time for me to become bishop. Yes, I was disappointed, hurt, and actually felt embarrassed that I did not win. I was humbled by the fact that I ran a stellar campaign. I put my pride on the sideline and asked God, "Okay, what is next for me?" I was reminded of a poem that I learned at Benedict College. Dr. Elizabeth J. Hart was one of my English professors, and I will never forget her eloquence when she recited her rendition of "A Dream Deferred" by Langston Hughes.

What happens to a dream deferred?
Does it dry up like a raisin in the sun?
Or fester like a sore—
And then run?
Does it stink like rotten meat?
Or crust and sugar over—
Like a syrupy sweet?
Maybe it just sags
Like a heavy load.
Or does it explode?

I have learned that God's delay is not His denial. He may not come when we want Him to, but He's always right on time! No, I did not win that election; however, I am eternally grateful that I followed God's plan for me. I accepted His challenge for me, and in accepting that challenge, I was able to meet so many wonderful and kind people from around the world. I had the opportunity to chair a mission trip to South Africa with a group of thirty-three participants. Seeking the position of bishop helped me to grow exponentially, spiritually, personally, and professionally.

God had more work for me to do at Union Bethel and in my personal life. Shortly after the 2008 General Conference, Union Bethel began to face some challenges that a new pastor would have had an arduous task of navigating. Sherita experienced an illness that required my undivided attention. There were family-related issues that surfaced that had to be dealt with. Today, several years later, I am once again a candidate for bishop. I rest in the assurance that God knows what is best for me and us. I am campaigning faithfully and preparing for the Forty-Ninth Session of the General Conference of the AME Church to be held in Nashville, Tennessee, in 2012. I go forth in faith, trusting God to order my steps. I am standing on His promises and trusting in His power. My continued prayer is that God will raise up God-fearing people who will pray for me and support my campaign through fund donations and volunteerism. This I do know: [God] is able to do exceeding abundantly above all that we ask or think according to the power that works in us, (Ephesians 3:20 NKJV).

A Prayer

December 21, 2011

Dear God,

Please make my crooked places straight, rough places smooth, and allow Your glory to be revealed in my life. Have Your way, dear God. I am not trying to tell You what to do or when to do it, but help me to trust You, for I know You will never hurt me or allow me to be put to shame. Use me and bless me to do Your perfect will. Thanks for a relationship with You. Thanks for never forsaking me or leaving me. I love You, and I will continue to do my best to trust Your plans for my life. Amen. Love, Harry.

CHAPTER NINE

Rest, Restoration, and Self-Care

A Prayer
May 25, 1995

Dear God, I went to the doctor today. My doctor says I definitely need to lose weight and begin light exercises. He also has me on a progressive medication to control my cholesterol. Lord, I can't lose this weight on my own. I need Your power. I am powerless. I need Your help, guidance, and direction. Please show me the way. Love Harry.

AS A PASTOR, how does one take care of oneself when so many competing forces are calling upon you every second, every minute, and every hour of every day? What do you do when you need a little time to rest, to rejuvenate, to relax? First Corinthians 6:19-20 states, "Do you know that your body is a temple of the Holy Spirit, who is in you whom you have received from God? You are not your own, you were bought at a price. Therefore, honor God with your body." Rest, restoration, and self-care are critical if you are going to survive as a pastor. How can you take care of others if you are not taking care of yourself? Self-care makes you a better caregiver. We only have one body, and how we treat this temple reflects on our overall happiness and well-being, not to mention our life span and immediate health. We also need to understand that there is a distinct difference between self-care and self-pampering or self-indulgence. Self-care has been defined as creating healthy lifestyle changes and developing stress management behaviors. Self-care means choosing behaviors that balance the effects of emotional and physical stress.

It was not until my close brush with death that I began to take care of my body and treasure it as a temple from God. As a young African American man, I should have been on point when it came to my health because of my family's history of high blood pressure, stroke, and heart disease. Taking time to care for yourself should remind you and others that your needs are important too. As a pastor and for people in general, having a well-cared-for body and mind can help you feel good about yourself, and if you feel good about yourself, it will reflect in all that you do. From the moment I became a pastor at twenty-one years of age, I neglected my own needs and did not know how to nurture myself, which lead to my bouts of *burnout*. It took me nearly dying before I got the wake-up call. That wake-up call clearly said that I had to begin taking care of myself. I had to find balance in my life, or everything was going to continue to spiral out of control. Over fifteen years ago, I made a conscious decision and started a regimen of self-care. My regimen began with me becoming more steadfast spiritually. No matter what is going on with me, I am going to find the time to pray, meditate, read the Bible, study with other spiritual leaders, and practice daily quiet-time routines to keep me connected to God at all times. Taking care of the spiritual me has helped me to maintain mental and emotional clarity and stability. I have organized myself and have created a daily schedule that balances work, relationships, recreation, and sleep.

At least three or four times per week, for a minimum of thirty-minute intervals, I exercise. I enjoy walking on the treadmill or doing power walks outdoors where I can commune with nature. Health professionals and experts highly recommend that we all exercise regularly to help us maintain our overall health.

REV. DR. HARRY L. SEAWRIGHT

Physical activity provides needed relief from stress. For those who continue to be reluctant to begin exercising, I encourage you to get started. It will change your life. Along with becoming more active physically, I also looked at what I was putting into my body. Changing my eating habits proved to be more difficult for me than starting an exercise routine. Remember, I am from the South, and I label myself as a true Southerner. I love traditional Southern food; however, to maintain a healthy diet, I had to adjust my eating habits. Remember, our bodies are temples of God, and we need to be aware of what we are putting into God's temple. As a part of keeping our bodies healthy and fit, for those of us who are on medication, I implore you to take your medication appropriately and speak with your physician about incorporating natural herbs into your health care plan. In addition to taking care of the physical you, you also need to take care of yourself mentally and emotionally, which involves finding time for yourself, family, and friends. As a pastor, you must impress upon your congregation the importance of valuing family and family time with them as well as protecting your personal "me" time. It is significant for the congregation of your church to respect your family and for them to be accepting in knowing that you were called to be the pastor, not your family. Setting boundaries with the congregation is essential when it comes to protecting you and your family as it relates to self-care.

The art of delegation is a wonderful tool. If God has placed people in your life with gifts and talents, by all means, use them. Don't be intimidated by people whose gifts and talents outweigh yours. Jealously, being insecure, and having little faith are major hindrances to the Kingdom of God. We must embrace all people. Yes, some will burn you, betray you and even hurt you. But we have to remember the goal is to win the Kingdom. I have found after 30 years of pastoral ministry, I have had more people to be a blessing than a hindrance.

Learning to share leadership is a great art. Exodus 18 (the story of Moses' advice to delegate) is the perfect example. In sharing leadership, I have found that good administration and organization can lead to mighty projects completed for the glory of God. I've learned over the years, the following actions are beneficial in preparing leaders to take on greater roles in the church: placing expectations in writing; producing manuals; enforcing sound teachings around biblical principles; organizing leadership retreats; recommending books to read on leadership; holding workshops and bringing in consultants, as well as encouraging members to find workshops and classes on their own, while paying for the cost of such. In the long run, you will witness a blessing to the ministry that will prove itself through growth and fresh ideas and innovative techniques that will bless the work of the church. I highly recommend listening to others' ideas, suggestions and concerns. Every meeting agenda should include a place for people to voice their ideas, suggestions and/or concerns. This method has produced many opportunities for growth and harmony. Every leader must strive to operate with integrity in all matters, particularly in the area of money matters. You should offer financial reports, monthly, quarterly and annually. If you can afford to have an audit of your church finances, then make it available upon request. Be approachable, compassionate and concerned. Remember, everybody is dealing with some issue and they want to know that you care about them. In other words, love the people and allow them to see your need for them and God. People do better, when they know better. They work harder, when they know they are appreciated and cared for. People want to come where they are loved and remembered. Know people's names; for our name is still the sweetest music to our ears.

Having good checks and balances will help you to serve with a sense of integrity and trust to any institution. Be as transparent as you can without embarrassing yourself and others. When our beautiful daughter got pregnant during her freshman year in college, it was a tremendous shock to us. Sherita and I felt like failures as parents. I was embarrassed and ashamed to even think about what people were going to say. We were hurt for our daughter, but we also knew she needed our full support and unconditional love.

When she decided that she was not having an abortion, we wholeheartedly made a decision to fully support her. She came back home from Benedict College in Columbia, SC (shout out to my alma mater) and we decided we would inform the church and ask for their love, support and prayers. What an outpouring of love, prayer and support we received. As a result of this request, many people confessed how they had been forced to have an abortion, left children with other family members, placed children up for adoption, and wished they could have been afforded that type of love and support.

Eight years later, we would not take anything for our grandson, Cameron Isaiah Seawright. He is a wonderful gift and declares that he is a preacher, just like his grandfather. He can pray, sing and speak with boldness.

We have faced my challenges as a family, but God's grace has been sufficient. Through our public and private struggles, we have learned that God does answer prayers and He has truly become our rock and high tower. We have learned to set boundaries, offer much unconditional love and have invited other people out of our family business. We have learned to not allow church members and other outside forces to talk about our family members to us. If you have a problem with Sherita, then go to Sherita; if you have a problem with me, then come to me. If you have a problem with our children, you come to us. We had to learn to send a message that if you mess with one of us, then you have to deal with all of us.

We try hard to live our lives beyond the congregation; we worked hard to create a life in our home beyond the church.

In other words, we try to do things as a family, outside the church. We took family vacations, normally places chosen by the children, we tried to carve out family nights and support each other to the best of our ability. One thing I am extremely proud of is for all the years our children were at home we had prayer every morning before they left for school. If Sherita or I were on travel, we prayed with them by phone. Rather than gifts, I would write letters to them. Even as adults, they remind me that they still have their letters.

I am proud of my children, Shari and Matthew. They have not done all we wanted them to do, and we have had some difficult times and events we have overcome, but I am glad to say they are very hard working people. Matthew is the operation manager in the cleaning company and Shari is employed by the District of Columbia's government. Once again, we have learned what unconditional love is all about and have learned that God's grace is sufficient for every weakness.

Living a life with purpose involves your being able to have confidence in others and delegating responsibility to them to help you be successful as a pastor. It is also important for you to realize that by delegating responsibility to others means that from time to time, people will fail. So be prepared when others fail you. It is not the end of the world, and God is in charge. Don't dwell on the failures of others. As part of your self-care, you need to cultivate friendships. Proverbs 18:24 tells us that "a man that has friends must show himself friendly." A true friend will hold you accountable.

A Prayer

January 9, 2007

Dear God, Lord, you are my dwelling place, my hope and assurance in times of distress and pain. You know just how much I can bear. Please help me to bear my load. Handle my business. God, you are my strength. You are my healer and miracle worker. God I praise You for your magnificent glory. Please help me this day, this hour and give me peace, hope and encouragement. God help us every day and every hour. Lord please hear my cry. I pray for obedience, deliverance, steadfastness and victory in every aspect of my life. Thank you God, Jesus and Holy Spirit for all you do. Love, Harry

CHAPTER TEN

Always Be Thankful

"Friendship is unnecessary, like philosophy, like art . . .
It has no survival value; rather it is one of those things that
give value to survival"

"Is any pleasure on earth as great as a circle of Christian
friends by a good fire?"

"The next best thing to being wise oneself is to live in a
circle of those who are."

Quotes by C.S. Lewis

I CONTINUE TO think back over my life, and I know that
God placed certain people in my life at critical times when
I needed them the most. It is important to always be thankful
to God for those who have made a difference in your life. I have
mentioned throughout this book several significant people who
have contributed to my life. I will continue with that list here. I
continue to thank God each day for so many friends who have
supported me and have been here for me over the years:

My wife, children, grandchild and other family members
College roommates, Fraternity brothers, business partners
My support group, prayer warriors, Prayer Line Participants
Fathers and Mothers in Ministry
Sons and Daughters in Ministry
Faithful friends over the years and their spouses

Bishops of the church

General and Connectional officers

Presiding Elders of the Second Episcopal District (Active and Retired)

Pastors of the Washington Conference

Pastors of the Second Episcopal District and the Connectional AME Church

Washington Conference, Second District and Connectional AME Church Laity

Board of Examiners Students, whom I taught and was Dean to for 10 years

Ecumenical Friends

Armor Bearers

A Prayer

June 9, 1995

Dear God, I thank You for today. I could have easily been the other way, but Your grace and mercy are so complete and real. I am just so grateful that You have allowed me another chance. Thanks for the love and support of so many of Union Bethel's members. The number of people who came to the emergency room was outstanding. I am so grateful. Dear God, thanks for how You are working everything out, opening mighty doors, pulling down strong walls and doing what needs to be done. Today was a blessed day. I saw my little girl (daughter) Shari graduate from sixth grade. God, You are good. Thanks for answering my prayer. Jesus, thanks for Your love. Love, Harry

CHAPTER ELEVEN

Don't Ever Underestimate the Power of Prayer

Notes on Grace

A S I CONCLUDE *Don't Faint: HELP for Hurting Pastors and Their Families*, I will share a few prayers and notes from my journal that I have kept through the years:

February 17, 1995

Life is bittersweet—ups and downs, joys, hopes, yet disappointments, unfulfilled dreams, temptations, lusts, evil desires, frustrations . . . the need to please. Today I finished reading the book *Just As I Am (E. Lynn Harris)*. This book has helped me see people who are different in a new light. I believe that God loves all people. All His children are special—gay, straight, bisexual, drunk, mentally disturbed, mixed-up, weird, young, old, rich, poor, weak, strong, black, white, yellow, red, or brown. God loves His children no matter what our flaws may be. What is the message I am preaching? Can people see my wounds?

February 27, 1995

God is good, and God is great. I thank Him for all His goodness, and I am forever indebted to my Savior, Jesus Christ. Today, Sherita and I celebrated thirteen years of marriage—a beautiful day. We had lunch at the Cheesecake Factory. Hope is in the air . . . A sense of love and commitment surrounds us. Bishop Adams called from South Carolina today inviting me to conduct a workshop next month. I am honored, joyful, proud, and a little overwhelmed, yet prayerful and grateful to God for this upcoming honor. My mind is racing, and I am concerned about getting out of the Prince George's Community College Board Retreat and the Men's Retreat at Union Bethel to be held the same weekend I have been asked to go to South Carolina. God, I am asking you to guide me through my cancellations, regrets and going to South Carolina. I am looking forward to seeing my mother and family. God, you are so good. Jesus is so good; the Holy Spirit is so good. Please continue to lead and guide me. My health is improving. Thank you, God.

June 15, 1995

Dear God, thanks for this beautiful day; a day of fishing with my son, Kevin Carter and his 2 sons. I am so very grateful for all that God has done for me. The Holy Spirit is a true comforter and provider. I thank Jesus my savior for Salvation and grace. Lord, I am still at a real crossroad in life. I want to start my consultant business. I want to become financial independent. I want to also assist churches in building buildings. I trust your faithfulness and timing. Help me to do the right thing every moment and every day. I believe you wholeheartedly for all that you do. Amen.

November 25, 1995

It always seems that I am at some crossroads in my life, a time when it seems that the load is too heavy, the burdens are too much to bear, or the work is too mighty. Please help me to always remember what I know in my heart that You are always near. Help me to know without a shadow of a doubt that You will always be here for me and that all I have to do is just trust You and believe in Your power.

Replace my fears with Your presence. Replace my doubts with faith. Replace my sadness with Your joy. Replace my hurt with Your tenderness. Lord, help me know that You will always answer my prayers. I can trust Your word and stand on Your promises. Thanks for being who You are, the one and only all-wise God who never fails. Amen.

January 8, 1996

Dear God, today is a beautiful snowy Monday, one of the largest snowstorms in the Washington, DC, area since 1979. I remember that snowstorm. Life is good. God, You are good. I thank you for the time to rest and time to be with family. Thank you for stopping us in our tracks and showing us how to slow down and take inventory of what is important. Help me to take advantage of this time to accomplish that which I need to accomplish. Thanks for Your love.

September 14, 1998

Dear God, life and all it fears; the fear of sickness, health, failures, death, problems with children, marriage, career, bills and meeting the challenges of life daily. This morning, I feel so tired, I hope nothing is wrong with my arteries. I pray for good health. I pray for strength. I am in a primary race I don't want to be in. I am disappointed by the lack of support I have received from the church and my friends. I am hurt, confused . . . I need you God to help me. God I really want to be a better parent, husband, son, and pastor. I am proud of the vision unfolding at Union Bethel and I truly thank God for allowing me to be a part of His move. You are so good and I truly pray for the best. Dear God, whatever you my Father holds, I want to always hold onto your unchanging hands. Thanks for being here for me. AMEN

December 28, 1998

Dear God, It's been a long time since I last actually wrote in this journal—my reflective thoughts-Life is so sweet. I am probably happier now than I have ever been in my whole life. It seems like the older I get, the more I enjoy life. I am so grateful for having a better understanding of your love, grace and will for my life. I have come to love and trust you so much more. I have come to trust and to depend on You for guidance, strength and encouragement. I am so grateful for my many blessings, my salvation, my wife, my children, my mother, sister, and brothers, in-laws, aunts, uncles, cousins, friends and my Union Bethel Church Family. I am so grateful for forgiveness, joy, hope, and the assurance of knowing that you are mine and I am yours. Thanks for all you do to make my life complete.

March 16, 1999

Dear God, today I am celebrating my forty-third birthday. Sherita just returned from Africa, and she had a wonderful time. I am very proud of her. I heard from several of my buddies: Rick, Kevin, and Melvin Greene. I spoke with my mother, and she is well. Sherita, Shari, Matthew, and I went to dinner at the Olive Garden. God, You continue to bless me. Sometimes, I become fearful when I see so many blessings being fulfilled in my life. Thank you, God, for all that You have done to make my life complete. I love You.

December 1, 2001

Dear God, there is so much going on in my life at this time. Matthew and Shari are not doing well in school. Shari is a freshman at Benedict College, Sherita's and my alma mater. I just returned from the Clergy Support Group Retreat in Atlantic City, New Jersey. I had a wonderful time, relaxing and enjoying myself. I feel restored. The support group thinks that I should run for bishop. God, I need to hear from You. Please give me clarity to hear Your voice. Thanks for Your guidance.

April 4, 2001

Dear God, thank you for your blessings. Thank you for your love, grace and forgiveness. Thanks for answering so many of our prayers—Sherita's book comes off the press today. The Brinkley Road construction project is going well. I saw it firsthand today. I feel so blessed, so protected and encouraged by you. Thanks for being who you are. Thanks, Jesus, for your love. Thanks Holy Spirit for your guidance and protection. Thanks for our friendship. Thanks for all you do to make my life complete. All that I am and all that I am not; I owe it to you, my glorious God.

January 14, 2002

Dear God, I have come to You on many occasions, sometimes crying and complaining. But today, I come to thank you for caring about me. You are so faithful. You have kept me, blessed me, and encouraged me. Thank you so much for bringing me through my fears, doubts, and worries. Forgive me for being faithless at times. Forgive me when I fail to trust You. Continue to be by my side. Teach me, O Lord, Your ways. You are my strength and my shield. Please continue to hear my prayers.

Today, despite all I have gone through, I will be a candidate for bishop of the African Methodist Episcopal Church. I have chronicled for you some aspects of my life: the good, the bad, and the ugly. It has not been an easy journey coming from the fields of Swansea, South Carolina, to the worldwide stage of being a candidate for bishop. God has blessed me, and He continues to do so. I am taking care of myself and getting the rest my body needs in order to continue His work. My suggestion to pastors is to find one day per week, one week per month, or one month per year for you to retreat in order for you to be a more productive and effective pastor and leader. Jesus retreated to pray, worship, and rest. He wants us to follow Him. It is no longer my will, but God's will I aspire to fulfill.

REV. DR. HARRY L. SEAWRIGHT

AUTHOR BIOGRAPHY

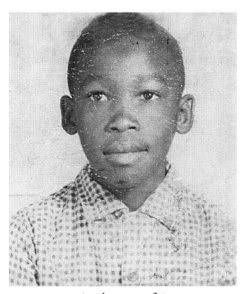

At the age of 8

| Walking across stage to receive Doctor of Ministry Degree | In wheel chair after being released from the Hospital the day before |

Sherita hooding me with Class by television.

Clergy Support Group 2004

Rev. Dr. Harry L. Seawright is the Pastor of Union Bethel African Methodist Episcopal Church in Brandywine, Maryland, where he has served since 1986. He is a native of Swansea, South Carolina. Rev. Seawright was called to preach in 1977; ordained as an Itinerant Deacon in the AME Church in 1979; and as an Itinerant Elder in the AME Church in 1981. In 1991, Rev. Seawright led the construction of the new $1.6 million sanctuary. Under **Rev. Seawright's** leadership and with God's anointing, Union Bethel has over 50 innovative ministries and 50 sons and daughters in ministry. In 2001, the Lord laid on his heart to start a satellite church in Temple Hills, Maryland and the Union Bethel Intergenerational Center, Inc. (IGC) was birthed. At this second church location, there are Sunday worship services, Church School, Intercessory Prayer, weekly Bible Study, and this facility is also a fully operational Day Care/Before and After Care Center that features a Banquet Hall for conferences, weddings, receptions and special events. The Center's mission is to "Foster Intergenerational Relationships and Strengthen Communities."

Rev. Seawright has spent over 30 years in ministry, specializing in community leadership, church construction and development.

He is a spiritual leader, business man, community leader, world traveler, author and a family man. Prior to becoming the pastor of Union Bethel AME Church, Brandywine, Maryland, in 1986, he was assigned as Pastor at Payne Memorial AME Church, Jessup, Maryland, from 1981-1983 and Hemingway Temple AME Church, Washington, DC, from 1983-1986. He is a Trustee Emeritus on the Board of Trustees for Prince George's Community College; President/CEO and Founder of HLS Consulting, Inc., a company that specializes in church construction, administration, management and finance and the Founder and CEO of We Kleen, Inc. a company of commercial cleaning, landscape and handyman services. He is also the CEO and Founder of the Union Bethel Intergenerational Center, Inc. (IGC) and the CEO and Founder of Prestige Realty, LLC.

Rev. Seawright's prophetic vision, outstanding leadership and visionary calling to led the Union Bethel AME Church membership into *'one church in two locations'*, has transformed the little church on the side of the road to a well-respected church serving over 1,500 members in the Washington Metropolitan area.

From five acres of land to now over fifty-five areas of land; from two employees to now over 75 employees; from a little chapel to a sanctuary that seats over 500; to property that includes three homes, an apartment, greenhouse, pond and so many other blessings, Rev. Dr. Harry L. Seawright knows the power of the Holy Spirit. He has not missed a day of reading his bible in over eighteen years. And anyone that meets him, knows, he is a praying man!

Rev. Seawright is the author of *More Than Bricks and Mortar: Building a Church Without Losing Your Mind*, 1996. He is a contributing author in *The African American Devotional Bible*, Meditation on Quality Leadership, 1997 and a contributing author in *The Pastor's Manual*, The Pastor's Role in Church Construction, 2000. He is been featured and quoted in the Afro-American newspaper, the Prince George's County Gazette, the Christian Recorder, The Washington Post, the Maryland Independent newspaper and local papers in cities that he visited to preach and teach.

He is Treasurer for the Washington Conference and the Second Episcopal District of the A.M.E. Church; the Treasurer of the 2nd Episcopal District Religious, Education and Charitable Non-Profit Board (RED, Inc.) and a member of the Collective Empowerment Group. **Rev. Seawright** is a member and past president of the A.M.E. Ministerial Alliance of Washington, D.C. He is the Founder and Past President of Bethel House, Inc., a nonprofit outreach ministry organization. During the 2008 General Conference, Rev. Seawright was a candidate for Bishop, were he ran a spirit-filled, spirit-led and spirit-driven campaign.

Education is very important to **Rev. Seawright**. He earned his *Bachelor's degree in Business Administration from Benedict College, Columbia, S.C. He earned the Master of Divinity and Doctor of Ministry degrees from Howard University School of Divinity.* As a member of the graduating class of 1995, he was awarded the Doctor of Ministry "Student of the Year." In 1996, he received the Concerned Black Christian Men of Prince George's County Religious Award; in 1998 he was listed in Who's Who in the Northeast. Rev. Seawright has recently been listed in the 2005-2006 edition of the National Register of Who's Who as a leading Executives and Professional. He attended St. Antony's College, in the University of Oxford, Oxford England in August 2004, where his presentation on "Dynamics of the Church, Politics and Education" was well received by the Oxford Round Table of distinguished leaders from around the world.

He resides in Fort Washington, Maryland with his wife, the Reverend Sherita Moon Seawright. They are the parents of Shari Nicole and Harry Matthew. And they are the proud grandparents of Cameron Isaiah.

CPSIA information can be obtained at www.ICGtesting.com
Printed in the USA
BVOW060315020512

289135BV00003B/4/P